AUTHOR

FREDERICK MARAIS RN MSc BSc (Hons)

From 1995 to 1997 Frederick Marais was employed by St. Mary's NHS Trust Hospital in London as TB/HIV Clinical Nurse Specialist to develop and manage a TB Service specifically for individuals co-infected with tuberculosis and HIV, and from 1997 until the end of 2000 as Manager & Lead Nurse to develop and manage a seamless Trust-wide Nurse-led TB Service.

During this time he undertook service planning visits to the Bureau of Tuberculosis Control, The City of New York Department of Health, New York City; TB Control Division, Department of Public Health, City and County of San Francisco; and to Tuberculosis Control, Health & Human Services Agency, County of San Diego.

He was very highly commended in the Medical Nursing category of the Nursing Standard Nurse 2000 Awards for his work in tuberculosis care and control. ▄

TUBERCULOSIS CONTROL

A NURSE-LED MODEL WITH CASE MANAGEMENT

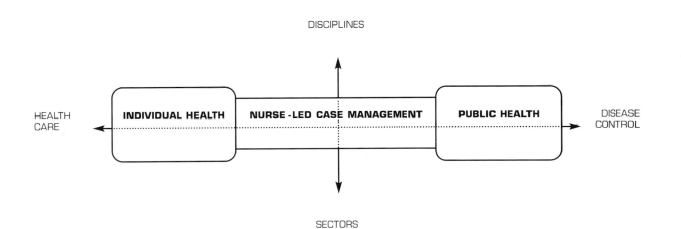

FOREWORD

The re-emergence of tuberculosis as a threat, both globally and in industrialised countries, has forced health care systems to review radically the way in which tuberculosis is controlled. The debate started in the late 1980's with the recrudescence of tuberculosis in the context of HIV disease in the USA. This quickly spread to European countries, the African sub-continent, South East Asia, and now the countries comprising the former USSR. Added to this, in the UK and similar European and North American countries, the effects of increased travel and migration have added further complexity to the tuberculosis dilemma, stimulating the generation of new models of care for the management of tuberculosis.

This book provides a clear, coherent and concise account of the generation of a new approach to the management of tuberculosis based on a multi-disciplinary, integrated, seamless approach involving all relevant stake-holders in a nurse-led and provided systematic framework. Frederick Marais, who comes from a senior nursing and academic background, is ideally placed to write this useful text describing a model of care in which he was intimately involved in generating and which is now being disseminated through the UK. Mr Marais came to the tuberculosis arena from a wide background of developing models of care from a nurse clinical practitioner background, predominantly in HIV disease, which has permitted in his work a broad and holistic approach to the multi-cultural and multi-societal dimensions involved in generating new models of care for the control of tuberculosis at the community level within the UK. This text provides a practical and theoretical framework which will be of value to nurses, doctors, community workers, social workers, people who work in the voluntary sector and healthcare planners alike. I commend this useful and concise text to the reader. ●

DR DAVID M MITCHELL M.A. M.D. M.B.A. F.R.C.P.
MEDICAL DIRECTOR, ST MARY'S NHS TRUST;
CONSULTANT PHYSICIAN, ST MARY'S NHS TRUST;
HONORARY SENIOR LECTURER IN MEDICINE, IMPERIAL COLLEGE; LONDON.

CONTENTS

>

NURSE-LED PROCESS 17

CASE MANAGEMENT 21

CASE MANAGEMENT – THE PROCESS 23

SERVICE-BASED ACTIVITIES:

OUTREACH ACTIVITIES:

EVALUATION 31

LIMITATIONS 35

RECOMMENDATIONS 37

CONCLUSION 40

DIAGRAMS 43

TABLES 47

ABBREVIATIONS

CCDC	CONSULTANT COMMUNICABLE DISEASE CONTROL
CNS	CLINICAL NURSE SPECIALIST
DOPT	DIRECTLY OBSERVED PREVENTATIVE THERAPY
DOT	DIRECTLY OBSERVED THERAPY
DOTS	DIRECTLY OBSERVED THERAPY SHORT COURSE
HA	HEALTH AUTHORITY
HIV	HUMAN IMMUNODEFICIENCY VIRUS
KCW	KENSINGTON, CHELSEA & WESTMINSTER
MST	MONTHLY SUPERVISED THERAPY
TB	MYCOBACTERIUM TUBERCULOSIS
WST	WEEKLY SUPERVISED THERAPY

SUMMARY

BACKGROUND

In London the incidence of tuberculosis continues to rise and there are multiple problems associated with programmes for effective control. At St. Mary's NHS Trust Hospital in central London the response to this important public health issue resulted in the development of a fully integrated Nurse-led TB Service with a Case Management approach. This model is recognised as an innovative approach, recommended to be implemented at other sites within the UK.

PURPOSE

Drawing on experiences in London and observations made in the USA, the purpose of this publication is to provide a descriptive and reflective account of the framework of a fully integrated Nurse-led tuberculosis control programme with a Case Management approach.

OBJECTIVES

1. To discuss the key factors demanding the need for change in tuberculosis service provision.
2. To describe the development, implementation and evaluation of a fully integrated Nurse-led tuberculosis control programme with a Case Management approach.
3. To highlight key achievements and existing limitations.
4. To propose recommendations.

OUTCOMES

This model for tuberculosis control provides the TB Nurse with an enhanced role. The TB Nurse, as Case Manager, is the interface for fully integrated individualised patient-focused care and effective tuberculosis control, functioning across traditional barriers such as those between medical specialities and hospital and community settings. This approach ensures continuity of care, sustains a consistent, co-ordinated and supportive approach and fosters adherence to treatment, promoting both individual and public health.

LIMITATIONS

At the moment there is limited available qualitative and quantitative evidence of the effectiveness of this specific model for tuberculosis control due to its novelty in the UK coupled with too few resources and insufficient investment. Formal research studies should be commissioned to assess the qualitative and quantitative impact on both individual and public health of a Nurse-led model with a Case Management approach.

CONCLUSIONS

There is a pressing need to review service provision for effective TB control. In some settings at least, a stronger focus on the central role of the nurse with a Case Management approach is workable and may produce highly effective results, but this approach demands sustained support and investment from key players.

BACKGROUND

The resurgence of tuberculosis (TB) and its emergence in new and potentially untreatable forms are continuing phenomena, threatening public health and control programmes world-wide. In London, tuberculosis notifications continue to rise and similarly the percentages of drug resistance, contrasting with rates in the rest of the UK. The proportion of notifications for England & Wales relating to London residents has increased from 29.0% in 1982 to 40.2% in 1998, and to 40.6% in 1999.[1] In addition, provisional data for the year 2000 show a rise of 10.6% over the last year for notifications in England & Wales, with two-thirds of the rise recorded in London.[1] During 1998, approximately 40% of culture confirmed tuberculosis cases were from London and of all multi-drug resistant cases in the UK, 46% from London; respective percentages during 1999 were approximately 58% and 39%.[2] At least fifty people per week develop active tuberculosis. Although tuberculosis is curable and preventable the mortality rates are high with an average of nearly two deaths per week. There are increasing levels of HIV-associated tuberculosis, socially excluded groups experience difficulty in accessing services[3] and failures in hospital infection control have led to nosocomial outbreaks of multi-drug resistant tuberculosis, again with high mortality levels.[4,5] In addition, compared with 15 other European cities, London has the third highest incidence rate.[6] Consequently, since the mid 1990s the TB Service at St. Mary's NHS Trust Hospital in London experienced increased activities, challenges and complexities in effective treatment, management and control of tuberculosis. ●

SETTING

The TB Service at St. Mary's Hospital has had to manage an ever increasing number of patients, the majority from disadvantaged socio-economic backgrounds. This became a changing profile demonstrated by the growing presence of patients who could not afford travel costs to access health or social care in either acute or community settings, an increasing number who lacked the financial means to purchase TB medication and/or food; all resulting in a demand for intensified nursing support and input with urgent referrals such as transport, social, legal and housing.

In addition to serving the local community in Westminster Health Authority (HA) with a population of 209,283,[7] St. Mary's attracts a large proportion of patients from other HAs because it is a major specialist centre for HIV/AIDS care and research, for paediatric infectious diseases and for tuberculosis care. It has a newly developed designated tuberculosis isolation unit with nine negative pressure rooms, it functions as a specialist referral centre for children and adults, it has a designated TB Service team (TB CNSs, Trust Lead TB Physician and Lead TB Physicians for medical specialities with a high TB caseload, and dietician), and it has an on-site TB laboratory with advanced diagnostic facilities and various planned TB-related research studies via Imperial College. Hence, the TB Service manages a significant proportion of patients resident outside the local HA, requiring innovative programme planning for care, adherence management and contact screening. For example during 1998, approximately 39% (n = 62) active cases and 40% (n = 19) chemoprophylaxis cases, and during 1999, 29%(n = 45) and 35% (n =22), lived outside the local HA.

Also, KCW HA contains large numbers of homeless people, including refugees and asylum seekers. There are particularly high concentrations of these groups within the hospital catchment area.[8] These are considered at high risk for a number of reasons: (1) arrival from a country where tuberculosis is endemic – in London, at least 55% of culture confirmed tuberculosis occurs in people born outside the UK and of those at least 35% arrived in the last five years;[3] (2) environmental and social factors such as poor housing and poor nutrition contribute to inequalities in health status and reduce resistance to disease;[9] and (3) poor knowledge of preventative services and difficulties in accessing care.[3]

Consequently, the TB Service at St. Mary's Hospital was experiencing increases in notifications and chemoprophylaxis [see Table 1.0, page 47]. At the same time the health and social needs of patients had become significantly more complex, resulting in a growing necessity for the implementation of supportive and adherence management strategies, such as Directly Observed Therapy (DOT), Directly Observed Preventative Therapy (DOPT), Weekly Supervised Therapy (WST) and Monthly Supervised Therapy. Yet, due to a lack of resources and insufficient investment in tuberculosis control in London, many TB Services do not have the infrastructure to sustain the delivery of effective adherence programmes.[10]

NEED FOR CHANGE

Previously, the TB Service at St. Mary's had been subject to various changes and had a prominent nursing input with marked service improvements.[11] However, the ongoing rise in tuberculosis incidence coupled with the identification of existing problems associated with programmes for effective care and control led to a need for yet further change, building on the contributions and improvements achieved by previous teams (nurses and doctors).

EVIDENCE FOR CHANGE

Rationale and evidence of need for further change which identified organisational and structural barriers to effective care provision, access and uptake, and to effective treatment outcome, disease control and health improvement, were obtained from:

- Audit, process and outcome evaluation.
- Integrated needs assessment and response (individual and population/community focus).
- Analysis of local, national and international research and surveillance data.
- Transdisciplinary and cross-sectoral discussions with health, social and community care providers.
- Consultations with patients and community organisations.
- Literature reviews.
- Information gathered during service planning visits to the Bureau of Tuberculosis Control Department of Health New York City, USA.

AUDIT, PROCESS AND OUTCOME EVALUATION

These measures were key steps documenting the existing need for change. For example, computer records of all HIV positive patients who were prescribed TB medication (full treatment and chemoprophylaxis) were obtained from the Hospital Pharmacy. The medical notes of this sample were audited, using several variables such as: notification date, prescription regime, duration of treatment, frequency of follow-up and by whom, duration and frequency of repeat prescriptions, accuracy of repeat prescriptions, adherence pattern and/or monitoring records, accuracy of changing to dual therapy, evidence and details of contact tracing and rationale for treatment or chemoprophylaxis. Data were measured against local protocols and national recommendations. In addition, the names of all these patients were cross-checked on the TB register to confirm that notification had been processed and by whom. Findings with recommendations were verbally presented to physicians and nurses within the HIV Directorate and discussed with TB Consultants.

SCOPE OF THE MAIN PROBLEMS

- The number of TB Nursing posts was inadequate for the caseload and these posts did not have an exclusive remit for tuberculosis care, other professional responsibilities at the time included chest medicine and non-tuberculosis related managerial duties.

- The TB Service was not integrated throughout the hospital and the team itself fragmented, one team for medical and one for HIV specialities.

- Not all patients were referred to and/or monitored by the TB Service, resulting in treatment errors, inconsistencies and poor adherence support and outcome evaluation.

- There was no nominated TB Lead Physician or Nurse.

- Within the TB Service there was no central TB Clinic for medical follow-up of patients.

- Overall service provision was patchy with patient care and adherence to treatment not consistently monitored or co-ordinated.

- Nursing documentation and patient information records were not standardised, not always accurate and up-to-date, and rapid evaluation of adherence/progress records were not always achievable.

- Effective adherence management was complicated because physicians were providing patients with multiple repeat prescriptions, at times patients were receiving incorrect prescriptions and treatment was changed or terminated inappropriately.

- Directly Observed Therapy was not offered as a standard of care.

- HIV discussion and, if required, testing were not provided routinely.

- Contact identification, tracing and screening details were not always accurately documented or cross-referenced with the index case.

- There was no forum for regular meetings between professionals involved in TB care.

- The TB Service did not have representation at the Hospital Control of Infection Committee Meetings, resulting in a low profile throughout the Hospital.

ADDITIONAL INFLUENTIAL FACTORS

Coupled with the main problems several other factors influenced the need for change. These included:

- Reports of nosocomial spread of tuberculosis in London.[4,5]

- Increased local burden of HIV-associated tuberculosis, paediatric cases, patients from deprived socio-economic circumstances, refugees, asylum seekers and homeless people.

- There was a greater awareness of the far-reaching impact on individual and public health including that of healthcare workers.

- Some foundations for enhanced TB control had already been established by previous improvements which were achieved following the appointment of a Specialist Nurse with specific responsibility for TB control at St. Mary's Hospital. [11]

- Cornerstones of this need for change were the consistent contributions, commitment and advocacy of past and present colleagues from various disciplines (e.g. Specialist Nurses, Chest Physicians and HIV/ID Physicians.

STRATEGY OF CHANGE

PURPOSE OF CHANGE

To reduce the spread and adverse health outcomes of tuberculosis by the development, implementation and evaluation of a Nurse-led TB Service with a Case Management approach – providing fully Integrated health and social care across disciplines and sectors.

RATIONALE FOR NURSE-LED/CASE MANAGEMENT

Rationale for the implementation of a Trust-wide Nurse-led Service with a Case Management approach as a strategy of change was attributed to critical consideration of influential factors, such as:

- Evidence of improvement in disease control following the appointment of a specialist Nurse with specific responsibility for tuberculosis care at St. Mary's Hospital.[11]

- Evidence of further improvements in TB service provision aimed at individuals co-infected with HIV following the implementation of a Nurse-led programme, managed by a TB/HIV CNS, within the HIV Directorate at St. Mary's Hospital.[12]

- Observations made and information gathered during service planning visits in 1997 to the Bureau of Tuberculosis Control Department of Health, New York City, USA.

- Evidence of the effectiveness and value of Case Management of tuberculosis control in the USA.[13-15]

- Following the identification of evidence of need for further change [see pages 7-8], coupled with the factors above, local consensus and support were achieved – between physicians (TB Consultants and TB/HIV Consultant), TB nurses and general/business managers – that a Nurse-led Service with a Case Management approach was the most effective strategy for seamless patient-focused service provision towards improved disease control, across disciplines and sectors.

WHAT IS A NURSE-LED SERVICE?

A Nurse-led Service is a service provision strategy assuring the transdisciplinary delivery and management of specialist patient-centred care with the TB Nurse as the pivot for effective individualised tuberculosis care and disease control across medical specialities and administrative boundaries; providing fully integrated health and social care in conjunction with medical and other health/social care providers, safeguarding both individual and public health. The role and practice of the TB Nurse, with Case Management as an integral part, foster the development of 'politically neutral partnerships' in care - with reference to the provision of specialist care in collaboration with different disciplines and medical specialities - reducing tensions over ownership of and authority for patient care [see Diagram 1.0, page 44].

INTEGRAL CORE COMPONENTS OF A NURSE-LED SERVICE

- **Nursing leadership:**
  - Nurses who are confident and competent with specialist skills, knowledge and expertise as prerequisites for effective Nurse-led Service provision, including Case Management.
  - Clear and agreed lines of management, responsibility and accountability.

- **Clinical leadership:**
  - Nurses with specialist knowledge, skills and expertise in order to practice effectively as autonomous practitioners and as part of a team, i.e. Case Management.
  - Comprehensive clinical group protocols, providing guidance and authorisation for the implementation of diagnosis and treatment protocols by the TB CNS team .
  - Physicians with specialist medical knowledge, skills and expertise.

- **Educational activities:**
  - Facilitated by specialist TB Nurses for nursing, medical and other health and social care providers towards effective patient care and disease reduction across disciplines and sectors.

- **Staff development:**
  - Nursing managerial strategies which foster ongoing support and opportunities for educational and professional development are essential for effective service provision.

- **Service development:**
  - Directed by the Manager/Lead TB Nurse but depending on the grading structure, each TB Nurse should have a defined level of responsibility.

- **Service management:**
  - Manager/Lead TB Nurse has overall responsibility for provision, administration and organisation of the service, but depending on the grading structure, each TB Nurse should have a defined level of responsibility and accountability.

WHAT IS CASE MANAGEMENT?

A systematic approach ensuring continuity of patient-centred care through the allocation of a nominated healthcare worker (TB Nurse Specialist) with clearly defined lines of responsibility and accountability. This person, the Case Manager, with the patient as the central focus, has prime responsibility for assessing, planning and delivering a consistent, co-ordinated, supportive and evaluative approach for effective tuberculosis management (care and control) from the patient's first point of contact with healthcare until successful completion of screening, medical investigation or treatment, discharge or transfer. This process fully integrates holistic health and social care across traditional and structural boundaries, specialities, disciplines and sectors. Tuberculosis management is both process and product in a Case Management approach – process evaluation is as important as assessing intervention outcome.

KEY STEPS FOR IMPLEMENTING CHANGE

KEY STEPS TAKEN FOR CHANGE
Various key steps were taken to introduce organisational and structural change, including:

- Support obtained for change, including implementation of a Nurse-led Service, from Nursing Director, Departmental Managers, Clinical Directors of medical specialities treating patients with tuberculosis and Public Health, through awareness raising and presentation of the scope of the main problems, lobbying and marketing of the projected positive contribution to patient care and disease control.
- Formal nomination of a Trust Lead Physician (Consultant) with overall responsibility for tuberculosis care and control.
- Appointment of a nurse as Manager and Lead Nurse with responsibility for the development and management of the TB Service.
- Nomination of Lead Physicians (Consultants) for medical specialities with a high incidence of tuberculosis - HIV, Paediatric and Renal Departments.
- Negotiation, collaboration and partnerships for shared and joint protocol/policy making, goals, responsibilities and ownership – transdisciplinary and across sectors.
- Development and promotion of the role of the TB Clinical Nurse Specialist (CNS) as a 'politically neutral partnership' in care.
- Establishment of a central TB CNS team, shared funding between Chest and HIV Departments.
- Protocol agreement allowing direct referrals to the TB CNS team.
- Protocol agreement for all inpatients commenced on treatment or chemoprophylaxis to be referred immediately to the TB CNS team.
- Protocol agreement for all tuberculosis notifications to be co-ordinated by the TB CNS team.
- Protocol agreement for all patients with TB to be reviewed periodically by the Trust Lead Physician.
- Protocol agreement for all patients with tuberculosis to be managed by a TB CNS.
- Development of specific protocols authorising the TB CNS team to implement diagnostic treatment.
- Development and implementation of designated TB Clinics at three Outpatient Departments - Chest, HIV and Paediatrics.
- Regular transdisciplinary feedback and, when required, readjustment of shared strategy for change.
- Endorsement by the Clinical Directors of relevant medical specialities.
- TB Service representation and membership on the Hospital Control of Infection Committee – ensuring service recognition at Trust level.

PROPOSED KEY STEPS FOR IMPLEMENTING A NURSE-LED SERVICE

Some of the following considerations may be helpful for the development and implementation of a Nurse-led Service, including Case Management:

- Ensure sustained political support – particularly resource investment, policies and multisector involvement - is essential to challenge and overcome institutional and professional resistance.

- Obtain support from Nursing Directors/Managers – e.g promote the benefits in terms of the quality of patient care and advancement of nursing practice, identify existing concerns/problems, and propose recommendations; use Clinical Governance, Hospital Objectives, Government Targets, etc. as yardsticks.

- Obtain support from key, and if possible all, physicians actively involved in TB management, across specialities – e.g. promote the benefits in terms of the quality of patient care and reduction in medical time/costs, and identify existing errors/problems; use Clinical Governance, Hospital Objectives, Government Targets, etc. as yardsticks.

- Obtain support from respective Business/General Managers - e.g promote the financial and service benefits, and identify existing problems; use Clinical Governance, Hospital Objectives, Government Targets, etc. as yardsticks.

- Obtain support from Public Health – e.g. promote the benefits in terms of assuring effective treatment of TB disease and preventing the spread of infection; use Clinical Governance, Public Health Objectives, Government Targets, etc. as yardsticks.

- In case of resistance to change, promote the advantage of a Nurse-led Service and the associated benefits to the Department/speciality concerned, in addition highlight the problems/errors in terms of patient care and disease control within that specific Department/speciality and propose recommendations; use Clinical Governance, Hospital Objectives, Public Health and Government Targets, etc. as yardsticks.

- Stress the benefits of continuity, consistency and co-ordination for sustained patient-focused support and care, across disciplines and sectors.

- Highlight the need for, and benefits of, a dual ongoing focus on both individual and public health.

- Emphasise the 'political neutrality' of a Nurse-led Service, i.e. fostering the development of 'politically neutral partnerships' in care with reference to the provision of specialist care in collaboration with different disciplines and medical specialities, reducing interdisciplinary tensions over ownership of and authority for patient care.

- Clarify that the TB CNS team works with, not for or against, medical teams with the shared goal of treatment completion and disease prevention, in line with agreed joint-protocols.

- Stress that physicians retain ultimate clinical and legal responsibility for patient survival, and that the TB CNS team practices in line with clinical protocols.

- Joint-policy/protocol making and shared goals across disciplines and sectors – ownership of and collective contribution to change are crucial for success.

- Regularly scheduled joint-reviews, allowing monitoring, evaluation and, when necessary, re-adjustment of goals – particularly assessing the impact of change on the workload of other specialities/disciplines, including the need for more resources, such as specialist nurses, physicians, isolation and diagnostic facilities, and other support workers.

- Clearly defined roles, responsibilities and accountabilities, including line management and funding structures, with formal endorsement at managerial/executive levels.

- Nomination of overall Lead TB Physician with formalised role responsibility and accountability, with endorsement at managerial/executive levels.

>

PROPOSED KEY STEPS FOR IMPLEMENTING A NURSE-LED SERVICE CONTINUED

- Appointment of Manager/Lead TB CNS with managerial and clinical responsibility and accountability.
- Development of the role of the Clinical Nurse Specialist in TB care and control.
- Strategy for staff recruitment, development, support and retention.
- Establishment of multidisciplinary and multisectoral forum, co-ordinated by the TB CNS team, for service review, development and improvement
- Strategic planning – i.e. vision, service specification, aims and objectives for service provision and future development, including actual and projected resource requirements, funding and specialist staff.
- Stress that the principles and processes of a Nurse-led Model with Case Management relate to those of Clinically Managed Networks.

STRUCTURE

INTEGRATED SERVICE PROVISION

Following restructuring, the framework of the TB Service now enhances the role of the TB Nurse as specialist healthcare practitioner with a specific remit for tuberculosis care and control and enables the nursing team to work effectively, integrating health and social care across traditional barriers such as those between different medical specialities and hospital and community services [see Diagram 2.0, page 45]. The management of patients is co-ordinated by the TB CNSs, ensuring the provision of a fully integrated seamless service across acute, outpatient and community settings; incorporating the management of adults and children, including those co-infected with HIV. This model, has been recognised as an innovative example in tuberculosis control,[21] It was based on a framework designed at St. Mary's for a specialist TB programme aimed at individuals co-infected with HIV,[12] incorporating aspects of previously established foundations for improved TB control.

ORGANISATIONAL

The service, situated within the acute sector, provides fully integrated Nurse-led care throughout the hospital and at three Outpatient Departments (Chest, HIV and Paediatrics), and also within the community setting. The TB Service has close collaborative working relationships with several specialities within the hospital (Microbiology, Pharmacy, Infection Control, Social Services, etc.), at local community level (Department of Public Health, Health Support Team Parkside Health and other community-based organisations), sector level (NW London Sector TB Programme), regionally (London TB Group) and nationally (Public Health Laboratory Services, TB Network Association, etc.).

TEAM MEMBERS

The TB Service team consists of a TB Service Manager [a TB CNS practising as Manager & Lead Nurse of the TB Service], three Clinical Nurse Specialists, the Trust Lead TB Physician and further nominated Lead TB Physicians within other specialities (HIV, Paediatrics and Renal). Due to a significant incidence of tuberculosis there is a link-TB CNS for each of these specialities for guidance, education, support and consultation. The input of a specialist TB/HIV Dietician is an integrated component of the team.

Clinical Nurse Specialist: Each TB CNS, in line with agreed protocols, is clinically accountable for his/her own actions, clinically responsible to the Trust Lead TB Physician, managerially responsible to the TB Service Manager, and professionally accountable to the Director of Nursing. The TB CNS team practices within agreed hospital protocols, working in close liaison with the Trust Lead TB Physician and other nominated Lead TB Physicians. Each TB CNS has a designated patient caseload, although the TB Service Manager has a smaller caseload enabling responsibilities for clinical leadership, service management and development. Specific job descriptions endorse the specialist role of the TB Clinical Nurse Specialist at Grades F & G levels [see Appendix 1.0, page 51].

The TB CNS team is responsible for statistics, represents the TB Service on the Control of Infection Committee at Trust level, and facilitates other multidisciplinary meetings in order to maximise patient care and interdisciplinary communication.

Potential new post of Therapy Support Worker: Following a successful six-month piloted project which provided adherence management (DOT, DOPT & WST) by a Registered Nurse on an outreach-basis [see Pilot project, page 27], a protocol and job description have been developed for a potential new post as 'Therapy Support Worker' (Healthcare Assistant Grading) [see Appendix 2.0, page 59, for Job Description]. The Outreach Therapy Support Worker will work in direct liaison with, and under the supervision of, the nursing team [See Diagram 3.0, page 46, for Team Structure]. However, due to extremely limited financial resources this post could be advertised only as a part-time position. Recruitement generated significant interest from both lay and community trained individuals and the position could have been filled had it not been part-time. Securement of political and managerial support for full-time funding remains a service objective, with the aim of cross-sectoral resource investment and capacity building.

Ethical framework: TB control raises various ethical implications and considerations for policy and practice, eg. patient confidentiality, respect for individual autonomy, public good versus individual good and differing personal, cultural and professional value systems. ■●

NURSE-LED PROCESS

The Nurse-led approach incorporates several integrated processes [see Diagram 2.0, page 45].

DIRECT REFERRALS

The TB CNS team accepts and makes direct patient referrals which are integral components of the Case Management process [see page 21]. This involves co-ordination and close collaboration with a variety of agencies including hospital-based medical specialities, community-based organisations, primary care, other TB Clinics, Public Health Departments and self-referred individuals. Urgent referrals, those who are TB symptomatic, are assessed immediately or on the next working day by a TB CNS in a fast-track service.

CONSULTANCY

TB CNSs are available for consultation by patients, public and other health and social care providers Monday to Friday via pager and telephone.

FIELD VISITS

As part of its remit the TB CNS team undertakes or, if not possible, co-ordinates visits within the local HA in order to trace individuals failing to attend screening or follow-up appointments, investigates sites of potential outbreaks of tuberculosis and screens contacts on site when unable to attend clinics. But, the ongoing lack of resources, specialist funding and staff, severely restricts all field activities.

HEALTH PROMOTION

Health promotion activities, both within acute and community settings, are focused on the individual, high risk groups/communities and health/social care providers. The theoretical frameworks which underpin health promotion strategies include health persuasion, legislative action, personal counselling and community development.[16] For example, training sessions could be held for health/social providers and service users within organisations working with local communities such as homeless, HIV and Somalian populations. Also, various health promotion leaflets have been developed for patients, the public and through the TB Network Association for a wider audience [see Appendix 3.0, page 63]. However, limited resources greatly restrain the frequency and evaluation of all health promotion activities.

EDUCATION

The TB Service has responsibility for the development, implementation and evaluation of multidisciplinary educational programmes within the hospital and also takes a lead in programmes to raise local awareness and contributes to national and international events. Within the hospital setting the TB CNS team has a prominent and leading role in transdisciplinary educational activities at ward and Departmental levels. For example, the team is an integral part of the hospital orientation programme for new staff nurses, provides educational sessions to physicians, Health Care Assistants and physiotherapists.

At local level, various educational sessions were provided for several community-based organisations, such as The Health Support Team and those working with homeless populations; and nationally, papers were presented at Royal College of Nursing Conferences and British Council Seminars. Further, the framework and activities of the Nurse-led TB Service were discussed at international conferences in the Channel Islands and Western Australia.

In order to raise awareness and to encourage collaborative working relationships between various disciplines within hospital and community settings and those directly affected by tuberculosis, the TB Service provided a Symposium on World TB Day during 1999 and 2000. On both occasions, these events were evaluated as extremely effective and essential for improved tuberculosis control.

Also, the TB Service plays a leading role in the development, delivery and evaluation of a specialist educational course in tuberculosis care and control at a local University.

SERVICE DEVELOPMENT

Evaluation: A vast amount of rich data are available in documented format but as a direct consequence of the lack of financial resources it has not been possible to conduct a formal research evaluation of the service. However, Case Management as an integral part of patient management ensures ongoing process, impact and outcome evaluation.

The involvement of service users in programme development is regarded as a goal for the TB CNS team. Accordingly a literature search has been conducted in order to develop a patient satisfaction assessment tool, for process and outcome evaluation, which could be incorporated as standard Case Management documentation.

Protocol & nursing role development: The TB CNS team is the key and takes a central leading role in the development of the nursing role and TB Service protocols/guidelines, jointly across disciplines and sectors.

Negotiation for joint-ownership and goals, including built-in review periods, is at the centre of this process. The TB CNS instigates and/or leads the preparation of guidelines in association with the TB CNS team, the Trust Lead Physician and other TB Physicians and Departments, such as Bacteriology, Pharmacy and Infection Control. Before final approval by the Trust Group Protocol Board comments are obtained from other key stakeholders in TB management, such as Public Health. The final structure and content is jointly approved – collective contribution and ownership are crucial for success.

Protocols are intended as a reference to provide guidance and authorisation for the implementation of diagnosis and treatment protocols by the TB CNS, working across specialities within hospital, community and community settings, enabling the provision of a Nurse-led Service. Protocols are reviewed annually and regularly evaluated. Improvements are incorporated based on research findings, service audits or other recognised national and international recommendations. This process ensures effective, research-based service delivery.

Partnership projects: The aim of the TB Service is to foster collaborative working relationships with local Primary Care Groups and other community-based health and social care providers, such as The Health Support Team within Parkside Health Authority. Patients are actively encouraged to contribute their experiences, their views of the quality of care received and recommendations for improvement to the planning, delivery and evaluation of educational events at hospital, university and community levels. Although these are currently not in written format, due to resource constraints, the ultimate aim is to formalise these contributions as part of service evaluation data.

Staff members: The key features of effective service provision are the expertise, commitment, enthusiasm and satisfaction of the team. Recruitment of appropriate staff and their subsequent development, dedication and retention have been identified as central priorities.[17]

Recruitment: Particular consideration has been given to develop specific strategies for staff recruitment, development, support and retention. All are regarded as an investment for service development and provision, with special attention to advertising, changes in person requirements and specifications, and a focus on comprehensive orientation and support structures.

Development, support and retention: At the point of joining the TB Service, a specific orientation programme is developed for each new staff member, according to individual level of expertise. Core educational objectives include: (1) introduction to, and support in the application of, the Case Management approach; (2) explanation of the structure and process of a Nurse-led Service; (3) clarification of the responsibility and accountability of the TB CNS as Case Manager; (4) time management and priority setting; and (5) the importance and legal implications of Case Management documentation. For those with no prior experience a short placement is arranged within the HIV/Sexual Health Department. The design, appropriateness and effectiveness of the orientation programme components are evaluated and adjusted accordingly, particularly the significance of the core objectives. The search is ongoing for an effective developmental structure to introduce and appropriately support the TB CNS practising within a Nurse-led Service and applying the Case Management process.

The TB Service Manager conducts team meetings weekly and one-to-one meetings monthly with each TB CNS to promote team dynamics, support individual development, and maintain commitment, morale and satisfaction. Each team member has an 'Individual Performance Review' contract jointly agreed between the TB CNS and the Manager, ensuring feedback, performance evaluation, and identification of developmental objectives. All staff members are encouraged to attend relevant educational and professional development courses and to undertake pertinent degree qualifications. Also, in addition to attending statutory Trust training days, a short course in self-defence training is provided on an annual basis.

Research: When possible, the TB CNS team contributes to quantitative and qualitative research studies, such as the incidence of HIV/TB co-infection[18] and the impact of respiratory isolation on patients.[19] Additional resources would enable the TB CNS team to initiate and conduct research on a more regular basis. ●

CASE MANAGEMENT

DEFINITION

As mentioned previously Case Management can be defined as: a systematic approach ensuring continuity of patient-centred care through the allocation of a nominated healthcare worker (TB Nurse Specialist) with clearly defined lines of responsibility and accountability. This person, the Case Manager, with the patient as the central focus, will have prime responsibility for assessing, planning and delivering a consistent, co-ordinated, supportive and evaluative approach for effective tuberculosis management (care and control) from the patient's first point of contact with healthcare until successful completion of screening, medical investigation or treatment, discharge or transfer. This process fully integrates holistic health and social care across traditional and structural boundaries, specialities, disciplines and sectors. Tuberculosis management is both process and product in a Case Management approach – process evaluation is as important as assessing intervention outcome.

KEY GOALS OF CASE MANAGEMENT

- **AIMS:**
- Assuring effective treatment of TB disease.
- Preventing the spread of TB infection.

- **OBJECTIVES:**
- Ensuring prompt and effective assessment, screening and diagnosis.
- Ensuring prompt accurate treatment intervention.
- Educating the patient.
- Rendering the patient non-infectious.
- Preventing the spread of tuberculosis.
- Preventing the progression of tuberculosis.
- Preventing drug resistance.
- Preventing relapse.
- Assessing for and prevent complications of drug contraindications and/or side effects.
- Assuring treatment adherence and effective treatment outcome.
- Searching for the possible source of tuberculosis infection.
- Identifying and screening others exposed to tuberculosis.

ESSENTIAL KEY COMPONENTS OF CASE MANAGEMENT

- Consistent care provision, by a designated person with identified responsibility and accountability.
- Establishment of supportive and trusting patient-care/therapeutic relationship for duration of treatment.
- Ongoing integrated assessment of individual risks, needs and strengths – health, personal, cultural and wider social influences on the achievement of health.
- Ongoing assessment of actual or potential barriers to effective treatment intervention, including structural and organisational factors (e.g. service accessibility, travel costs and payment of TB medication).
- Identification of needs and goals in partnership with the patient.
- Planning and implementing health interventions, responses for the achievement of health (i.e. connecting the patient with the resources, e.g. referrals, incentives/enablers and outreach DOT).
- Provision of support and encouragement for duration of treatment.
- Co-ordination of care for the duration of treatment.
- Health promotion, educating patients and their contacts, plus other health and social providers.
- Advocacy for the patient and for improved tuberculosis care and control in general.
- Ongoing monitoring and evaluation of treatment progress and adherence.
- Documentation - comprehensive, accurate and up-to-date.
- Focus on improved individual and public health.

KEY ATTRIBUTES OF AN EFFECTIVE CASE MANAGER

- Knowledgeable:
  - Understands the principles of tuberculosis prevention, screening, diagnosis, care, treatment and control.
  - Awareness of the impact of structural barriers to the spread of disease and achievement of health, including organisational and wider social factors.
- Skilled
  - Specialist clinical nursing skills and competencies in tuberculosis management.
  - In advanced nursing practice in line with agreed clinical/group protocols.
  - Ability to practice autonomously and as part of a team.
  - In setting priorities and time management.
- Educator:
  - Facilitates effectively education at the level and ability of the target audience.
- Communicator:
  - Effective communication skills, oral and written.
- 'People skills':
  - Ability to relate well to others, regardless of social status, culture, ethnicity, etc.
- Counselling skills:
  - Provides counselling and ongoing support and encouragement.
  - Deals effectively with sensitive issues, such as HIV, sexuality, gender issues, etc.
- Facilitator:
  - Ability and confidence to negotiate, co-ordinate and liaise effectively with patients and other providers.
- Evaluator:
  - Monitors/evaluates continuously patient progress, and treatment adherence.
- Administrator
  - Keeps accurate and up-to-date patient records, documents and reports.
- Advocacy skills:
  - Advocates for the patient and improved tuberculosis care and control in general.
- Reflective:
  - Ability to reflect critically on own practice and service provision.
- Researcher:
  - Ensures the collection of high quality clinical data to facilitate effective monitoring and evaluation..

CASE MANAGEMENT: THE PROCESS

Case Management incorporates several integrated processes [see Diagram 2.0, page 45].

KEY STEPS IN CASE MANAGEMENT

- Receipt of direct referral.
- Allocation of Case Manager.
- Contact patient and conduct integrated capacity assessment, including resources, needs and risks.
- Conduct screening and/or co-ordinate medical investigation and follow-up.
- Ongoing management – regular contact, evaluation, follow-up and support - until completion of screening, medical investigation or treatment, discharge or transfer.

SERVICE-BASED ACTIVITIES:

NEW REFERRAL & CASE ALLOCATION

The TB CNS team is notified with details of all inpatients, outpatients and those in the community. On referral, all contacts, individuals requiring further investigation for possible tuberculosis, patients on treatment and those on chemoprophylaxis are allocated a Case Manager (TB CNS) and remain with the Case Manager until discharge. Each Case Manager, including the TB Service Manager (TB CNS) has a designated patient caseload. In order to provide safe and effective individualised tuberculosis care and control, Case Management experience at St. Mary's Hospital would suggest a minimum of one nurse per case load of twenty-five to thirty if the Case Manager has full admin and secretarial support and is not routinely responsible for administering DOT/DOPT [see Level of Nurses, page 36]. However, in practice, due to limited resources, Case Managers have to manage much larger caseloads ranging from forty to sixty and above, with possible negative implications for safe practice, staff morale, individual and public health. The TB Service Manager has a smaller caseload enabling responsibilities for clinical leadership, service management and development.

PROCESS

In line with agreed hospital protocols, each Case Manager is responsible for ensuring successful completion of investigations and/or effective treatment outcome and preventing the spread of infection. This process may involve referral to other professions and/or organisations, but the Case Manager is ultimately the key to effective co-ordination. Case Management ensures continuity, a consistent, co-ordinated and supportive approach and fosters adherence to treatment. It involves the following core processes:

Documentation: Comprehensive, accurate and up-to-date patient records, documents and reports are crucial for effective Case Management, also ensuring easy cross-cover for continuity of care by the TB CNS team during absence of the actual Case Manager.

A detailed documentation system has been developed allowing rapid access to current information about each case for all disciplines e.g. laboratory and bacteriology results, sensitivity patterns, prescribed drugs, side effects, adherence records, progress, referrals to other services, follow-up arrangements and personal details of all identified contacts. The documentation has been designed to enhance quality of patient care through improved communication among multidisciplinary team members and to identify potential barriers to effective treatment outcome.

Documentation for each referred individual is kept in a separate file within the TB Service. These files, TB Nursing documentation, are utilised by all disciplines for up-to-date and accurate information regarding individual Case Management care plans. Following discharge, these notes remain within the TB Service for future reference.

Risk assessment: Specific documentation has been designed as a comprehensive risk assessment tool for the evaluation of new referrals. For example, each referred patient is assessed for signs and symptoms of tuberculosis; previous treatment, including preventative therapy; and risk factors, including country of origin, living circumstances, employment status, drug/alcohol dependency, any previous incarceration, and general medical condition. The association between HIV and tuberculosis is discussed routinely with contacts and HIV testing is actively pursued with those on TB treatment. In order to increase uptake and continuity of care, following training of all TB CNSs, HIV discussion and testing are to be conducted as a standard of care by the Case Manager when risk assessment identifies an increased risk of HIV co-infection, also recommended by the British Thoracic Society.[20] A recent study at St. Mary's Hospital reported a 24.8% rate of co-infection[18] in all TB cases. In addition, co-infection with HIV and tuberculosis has been reported as an issue for some in London, particularly those communities from African countries.[21]

Screening: Following risk assessment, the Case Manager will proceed with clinical screening in line with protocol. Specific guidelines have been developed for the screening of children of various ages, individuals co-infected with HIV and those not knowingly co-infected. Clinical procedures as part of TB Nurse screening include: Heaf/Mantoux testing, CXR, blood tests (e.g. FBC, LFT, CRP, ESR) and requesting sputum specimens. TB symptomatic cases are referred immediately to a TB Physician – depending on the origin of the initial referral this could be to either the Trust Lead TB Physician or to one of the nominated Lead TB Physicians if the patient is from within their speciality (HIV, Paediatrics or Renal). Others could be referred either for medical consultation or discharged in line with protocol.

Notification & contact tracing/screening: New cases are referred directly to the TB CNS team for notification. Local policy reinforces this practice. Systems are in place which ensure that the TB CNS team is notified immediately by Microbiology with all positive results, ensuring prompt action. In addition, culture and other results suggestive of tuberculosis are sent directly to the TB CNS team and records of patients prescribed anti-TB medication are obtained monthly from Pharmacy. These records are examined and 'unknown' cases investigated and notified. A cross-checking system minimises the risk of under-notification and ensures all patients are included in the system.[11] As an illustration retrospective cross-checking in 1996 revealed a total of five cases which were not notified during the previous year. The Nurse-led approach has significantly improved the notification rate to 100%, by cross referencing computerised clinical diagnostic and pharmacy records for the whole hospital. This includes cases co-infected with HIV/TB which are commonly not notified, due to concerns about HIV confidentiality and the statutory required notification of tuberculosis.[22, 23]

The respective Case Managers have responsibility to ensure the identification, tracing, screening, treatment intervention and evaluation of contacts. The local Consultant in Communicable Disease Control (CCDC) is routinely notified of any contacts failing to attend assessment on more than one occasion, of those resident outside the local area and those in any potential high risk situation, e.g. mass screening involving homeless people, children or those with HIV.

Case follow-up: In-patients commenced on treatment are notified immediately to the TB CNS team and visited frequently by their Case Manager, especially those in respiratory isolation, to establish a supportive relationship. The Case Manager plays a most important role from the patient's first point of contact with tuberculosis healthcare (investigation or treatment) and beyond, a resource for consistent support and comprehensive information on hospital, community and public health measures.[19] This is a crucial component of Case Management because the initial healthcare experience, and the associated attitudes and feelings of being hospitalised are major contributing factors to the patient's acceptance and participation in ongoing tuberculosis treatment.[24,25]

All patients, including those on chemoprophylaxis, are followed-up and supervised by the respective Case Manager at least monthly (MST). Nursing consultation includes visual acuity and colour blindness testing, monitoring of progress, assessment for side effects, repeat blood testing, evaluation of treatment adherence and management and provision of repeat medication. As a standard of care, patients are provided with monthly repeat prescriptions, co-ordinated by the Case Manager and dispensed from St. Mary's, allowing close adherence monitoring and eliminating repeat prescription errors. Patients are advised not to attend their GPs for repeat prescriptions unless in an emergency. In line with protocol, physicians are requested not to provide repeat TB prescriptions without informing the TB CNS in order to ensure accurate and consistent adherence monitoring. Recently, a protocol has been agreed authorising the TB CNSs (Grade G and above only) for the management of continuation treatment prescriptions, thereby improving continuity of care, treatment adherence and reducing waiting times during follow-up.

Implementation of this protocol has had to be postponed due to nursing and pharmacy staff shortage. Those with uncomplicated tuberculosis are seen routinely by TB physicians at diagnosis and at initiation of treatment, at the commencement of dual therapy and at completion. Medically complex cases are referred to physicians according to TB CNS assessment and individual care plans.

Outpatient Clinics: These include the provision of several specialist Nurse-led Clinics at three Outpatient Departments: (1) Walk-in Screening Clinics with no appointment required; (2) Follow-up Clinics; including adherence management; (3) Paediatric TB Clinic; and (4) HIV/TB Clinics. Also, there are combined Nursing/Medical Clinics: e.g. Follow-up and New Referrals for medical patients, children and those co-infected with HIV. To maximise flexibility and accessibility special arrangements are made for rapid assessment via a fast-track service of urgent referrals and those on treatment who cannot attend within the allocated clinic hours.

Adherence – clinic appointment: The Case Manager is responsible for monitoring the adherence of every patient on a continuing basis. The following action is taken when a patient fails to attend an appointment: an immediate phone call is made to the patient and another appointment arranged if the patient has sufficient medication; if not reached by phone, a home visit is undertaken by the Case Manager or, if possible, by community-based healthcare workers already involved in the care of the patient. If all attempts are unsuccessful, the CCDC will be informed and several further attempts will be made to contact and return the patient to service.

Treatment adherence management: Various strategies have been implemented in order to monitor treatment adherence: Case Management, monthly follow-up by the Case Manager, monthly repeat prescriptions co-ordinated and managed by Case Managers, tablet counts, urine checks, home visits if the patient fails to attend follow-up, establishment of a supportive patient-carer relationship and a record of attendance and patients' descriptions of their adherence patterns. Specialist documentation has been developed for this purpose allowing rapid evaluation of individual adherence records. In addition, nursing assessment by means of the Case Management documentation helps to identify and overcome possible barriers to treatment adherence. For example, a patient may be street homeless, mentally unstable, alcohol or drug dependent, impoverished, living in poor accommodation or personally or culturally in need of assistance.

As a result of expanding the Nurse-led approach, DOTS, DOPT and WST are now available as a standard of care, enabling Case Managers to increase support further and to encourage completion of treatment. Those requesting enrolment, or those encouraged by the Case Manager, are offered a choice of three strategies: (1) clinic-based: assistance with travel costs can be provided; (2) community-based: co-ordinated by the Case Manager but delivered by other healthcare workers, e.g. District Nurses, Health Visitors or Community-based Outreach Teams such as The Health Support Team; (3) and when medically crucial and as a last resort, due to the lack of resources, on an outreach-basis: provided by the TB CNS team. When community-based healthcare workers manage patients, the Case Manager acts as co-ordinator, providing support and monitoring their intervention [see Adherence Management, page 26 and 36].

These adherence management strategies are still being refined according to local needs and the effectiveness of the various strategies closely monitored. However, availability of resources dictates levels of provision, access and uptake. For example, lack of resources lead to the temporary suspension of all outreach strategies in November 1999, resulting in a small number of cases managed only by means of clinic-based interventions. Consequently, those identified as in need of outreach adherence supervision could not be supported or monitored and had to self-medicate, a cause of concern for both individual and public health.

Positive results of a six month pilot project during 1999 which provided adherence management by a Registered Nurse on an outreach-basis [see Pilot project, page 27] resulted in the development of a proposed unique post as 'TB Therapy Support Worker' (Healthcare Assistant Grading) [see Appendix 2.0, page 59, for Job Description].

Case Management meetings: The TB CNS team and TB physicians hold weekly meetings to update patient adherence and progress and to plan rapid action when needed.

Activity sheet: A specifically designed tool, allowing each TB CNS to record on a daily basis individual Case Management and service activities. This sheet, part of the document system and kept on file, reflects several variables, allowing monthly statistical breakdown relating to patient management and general service provision, e.g. total number of patient episodes, site of follow-up (i.e. outpatient, inpatient and/or community) and medical speciality.

OUTREACH ACTIVITIES

STAFF SAFETY
Violence and threats of violence directed toward public health outreach-workers are common occupational hazards.[26] Accordingly, specific protocols have been developed to maximise the safety of team members during outreach assignments [see Appendix 4.0, page 69] and for the transportation of anti-TB drugs [see Appendix 5.0, page 73]. In addition to several key measures, including the use of mobile phones and notification of expected time of return, a basic course in self-defence training is offered on an annual basis.

FIELD VISITS
Another aim of the service is for the respective Case Manager to visit patients within the first month of commencing treatment, including those on chemoprophylaxis, at home, hostel, shelter, etc. This allows the development of an open, honest and supportive patient-carer relationship; assessment of health and social needs; identification of barriers to adherence; evaluation of progress and treatment adherence; confirmation that all contacts have been identified; further education for patients and families/carers/friends about tuberculosis, its treatment and side effects; and for those who fail to attend appointments, an encouragement to return to the service. Unfortunately, due to the lack of resources and an increasing caseload, this aim is not always achievable. Further, problems in obtaining rapid interpreter services, coupled with linguistic incompatibilities of staff, result in delayed responses.

ADHERENCE MANAGEMENT
Depending on available staff resources, from within either the TB Service or community (such as District Nurses,

General Practitioners, Schools, Pharmacies, etc.), DOT, DOPT, WST and MST strategies can be provided at any mutually agreed venue – e.g. at home, school, work or even in a public place.

Ideally, the TB Service itself should provide an outreach adherence management programme to ensure consistency, continuity and ongoing specialist support, encouragement and evaluation. Unfortunately, this is not possible due to lack of investment in TB control. Consequently, the Case Manager initially endeavours to establish a partnership with a community-based organisation to provide the chosen adherence strategy. In such circumstances the Case Manager acts as co-ordinator, providing support and information, and monitoring the intervention of the provider. In addition, the Case Manager secures, in writing, an agreed contract with the provider, clarifying and confirming responsibility and accountability and action to be taken in the event of unsuccessful intervention. However, it is extremely time consuming and difficult to establish such collaborative partnerships because community-based workers are increasingly unable to take on this added responsibility due to their own expanding case loads, professional remits and lack of resources. Therefore, as a last resort and when medically crucial, the TB CNS team will try to provide an outreach service but due to the lack of resources, coupled with a growing need for outreach strategies, this is often not sustainable.

PILOT PROJECT

During 1999, a project which provided adherence management (DOT, DOPT & WST) by a Registered Nurse on an outreach basis was successful piloted for a period of six months, with an average caseload of thirteen patients per month. At the time, the project was established in answer to a growing need for adherence support, encouragement and supervision. Support for this pilot was obtained through a comprehensive written analysis, presented by the TB CNS team to managerial/executive levels, stressing the associated costs and safety risks of patients attending clinic-based adherence. Variables for analysis included: (1) the degree of disruption of family routine having to co-ordinate and attend separate hospital appointments for adults and children, resulting in attendance and treatment failures; (2) the total costs for provision of travel expenses; (3) frequency of stigma and victimisation displayed by neighbours towards patients when hospital transport was provided, leading to anxiety and fear, resulting in attendance and treatment failures; (4) the occurrence of relapse, readmission and associated treatment cost; (5) inability to guarantee the physical safety of children attending a busy clinical hospital environment; (6) and the level of unsuccessful adherence management provision by community-based health care workers, unable to take on and/or sustain the associated responsibilities due to their own expanding case loads, professional remits, and lack of resources and awareness of the rationale for adherence supervision.

The provision of such an outreach adherence programme was a new strategy for the TB Service and was closely monitored. As an integral component of Case Management, the Outreach Nurse and patients were asked informally to provide feedback about their experiences and the perceived benefits and limitations of providing/receiving support with therapy on an outreach basis [see below]. This feedback confirmed its success – patients found it acceptable and noted its values of support, accessibility, flexibility, continuity, consistency in care provision, and as holistic in terms of response to health and social needs. From a service provision perspective, this approach increased quality and standards of care, thereby promoting effective treatment outcome. This reduced costs by minimising travel expenditure and by preventing relapse, readmission, and spread of infection. It also increased staff satisfaction, motivation and morale. However unfortunately, due to lack of funding this project had to be suspended after a period of six months. Consequently, those identified in need of outreach adherence supervision could not be monitored and had to self-medicate, putting the achievement of individual and public health goals at risk.

The development of a protocol and job description for a potential new post as 'Therapy Support Worker' (Health Care Assistant Grading) was a further positive outcome of this pilot project [see Appendix 2.0, page 59, for Job Description]. Specific consideration was given to various details, including: training requirements and support; working background and experience; professional boundaries, responsibility and accountability; legal issues; and pharmaceutical and group protocol mandates. It is anticipated that the Outreach Therapy Support Worker will work in direct liaison with, and under the supervision of, the nursing team [see Diagram 3.0, page 46]. This post will play a central role in the treatment of individuals with tuberculosis, adults and children, including those co-infected with HIV, across hospital and community settings. The Therapy Support Worker will provide care in partnership with the TB Clinical Nurse Specialist Team and will be responsible for delegated elements of the adherence management care plan of patients. Recruitment was attempted, but however was unsuccessful due to extremely limited financial resources.

The pilot project received feedback from both patients and the Outreach Nurse, this is demonstrated in the charts below.

FEEDBACK FROM PATIENTS/SERVICE USERS: OUTREACH THERAPY SUPPORT PILOT PROJECT

EVALUATION METHOD

Due to lack of funding it was not possible to conduct formal outcome evaluation research of the impact and outcomes of the project. Nevertheless, in addition to process and outcome evaluation, integral components of Case Management, patients were asked informally by the Outreach Nurse about their experience, the perceived benefits and limitations of receiving support with therapy on an outreach basis. Views expressed were recorded, similar and recurrent themes clustered in main categories.

> **BENEFITS**
> - Flexible service provision and access enhances support and encouragement for adherence with therapy.
> - Response to the patient's personal, social, economical and geographical circumstances.
> - Preventing or limiting fragmentation and disruption of family lives – family unit supported together, preventing multiple appointments at various times during the day/week.
> - Decreasing stigma – hospital/clinic appointments raise anxiety for some regarding confidentiality.
> - Continuity and consistency in service delivery by the same person increase trust in the healthcare system and openness regarding notification of poor adherence and other health/social problems.
>
> **LIMITATIONS**
> - Service provision during day time only.
> - No early morning service, especially for children before going to school.
> - No weekend service.

FEEDBACK FROM OUTREACH NURSE: OUTREACH THERAPY SUPPORT PILOT PROJECT

- **BENEFITS**
- Continuity increases understanding of the personal, social and cultural needs of patients.
- Enhancing patient-carer relationship, leading to a higher degree of mutual trust.
- Getting to know the patients very well, maximising a positive treatment outcome.
- Health promotion – ability to assess and address barriers to effective treatment, preventing negative impact on treatment and health outcome.

- **LIMITATIONS**
- Time consuming – travelling by public transport to and from destinations.
- Becoming too involved – tendency to take on more than health and social needs.
- Frustrating – difficulty travelling to and from destinations and not finding patients at home.
- Tiring – travelling by public transport, and some patients especially children, require intense and ongoing support and encouragement.

CONTACT INVESTIGATION & SCREENING

Under the direction of, and in collaboration with, the local CCDC, the TB CNS team conducts all investigations and risk assessments of possible cross-infections and outbreaks in the community. To increase access and uptake, particularly among 'hard-to-reach', vulnerable and marginalised groups, screening can be offered on an outreach basis, depending on individual circumstances. For example, on-site screening, including risk assessment, Heaf testing and CXRs, were provided recently at an organisation working with homeless populations. ●

EVALUATION

Due to lack of resources, funding and staff, it has not been possible, to date, to conduct formal outcome evaluation research to establish the full impact of a Nurse-led TB Service with Case Management approach on tuberculosis care and control. However, its implementation has led to several major achievements in service organisation and delivery [see below] and in treatment outcome [see Table 2.0. page 48, and Table 3.0, page 49]. Also, feedback from service users and other disciplines indicate its success and feasibility for health improvement [see pages 33 & 34]. In addition, data from a research project, studying the impact of respiratory isolation on patients, highlighted the value of the role of the TB CNS.[19]

Further, although not formally researched, from observation and basic calculations it could be anticipated, that cost reduction could be an additional achievement. For example, (1) direct referrals to TB CNS team, resulting in reduced waiting time for assessment and clinical intervention; (2) fewer medical consultation appointments; (3) prevention of prescription duplications and errors; (4) intensified and ongoing follow-up, support and adherence monitoring, preventing relapse, drug-resistance and spread of infection; and (5) TB CNS profile, practice and availability for clinical consultancy, guidance and support throughout hospital, minimizing risk of nosocomial spread of infection. This framework of service provision for TB care and control continues to be developed at St. Mary's Hospital and is recognised as an innovative example of TB control and recommended to be implemented at other sites. [3, 21, 37]

MAIN ACHIEVEMENTS OF NURSE-LED MODEL WITH CASE MANAGEMENT

Service restructuring resulted in several key achievements in service organisation and delivery, including:

IMPROVED PATIENT CARE

- Provision of specialist nursing care, integrating health and social care across medical specialities, diciplines and administrative boundaries.
- Specialist TB care provision within and across hospital, outpatient and community settings.
- Sustained support and encouragement for duration of treatment.
- Increased notification rate.
- Improved treatment completion rates.
- Direct referrals to and assessment and screening by the TB CNS team.
- Fast-track service with nursing consultation immediately or next working day.
- More flexible service provision, responding to the needs of patients.

>

IMPROVED PATIENT CARE CONTINUED

- Minimised disruption of patient's individual daily routine and/or family lives.
- Nursing management of repeat prescriptions, preventing errors and duplication plus ensuring continuity, consistency and accurate adherence monitoring.
- Development and evaluation of tuberculosis related health promotion information.
- Standardised HIV discussion and, when requested, testing.
- Service user involvement in awareness raising and service development and evaluation.

ADDITIONAL ACHIEVEMENTS, IMPROVING PATIENT CARE

- Trust-wide seamless Nurse-led service provision.
- Improved practice across specialities and disciplines, through joint service planning and policy making.
- Development of the role of the Clinical Nurse Specialist in TB care and control.
- Nominated Trust Lead Nurse and Physician.
- Nominated lead TB physicians within medical specialities with a high incidence of tuberculosis – such as HIV, paediatrics and renal services.
- Variety of Nurse-led clinics within three Outpatient Departments.
- Link-TB Nurse for medical specialities with a high incidence of tuberculosis for support, education and consultation to change/improve practice.
- Standardised specialist nursing documentation.
- Documentation for rapid adherence, progress evaluation and research.
- Comprehensive and standardised adherence management strategies.
- Cost reduction (anticipated, as discussed in Achievements & Evaluation, page 31).
- Enhanced collaborative working relationships with Primary Care and other community-based organisations.
- Symposia on World TB Day in 1999 & 2000.
- Educational partnership with a local University.
- Integral part of, and leading role in, hospital-based transdisciplinary educational activities.
- Development, implementation and evaluation of nursing and transdisciplinary protocols.
- Role and protocol development for post of TB Therapy Support Worker (non-nursing).
- Protocol development for the management of repeat TB prescriptions by the TB CNS team.
- Working towards partnership projects, e.g. with a local Primary Care Group.
- Quarterly TB Service meetings - transdisciplinary.
- Membership of the Hospital Control of Infection Committee.
- Activity sheets, allowing daily recording and statistical breakdown of Case Management and service activities.
- Strategy for nursing staff recruitment, development, support and retention.
- Staff expertise, commitment and ongoing professional development.

FEEDBACK FROM SERVICE USERS & PATIENTS: NURSE-LED SERVICE & CASE MANAGEMENT

EVALUATION METHOD

Feedback, comments made and views expressed by service users, including by patients during the Case Management process, were recorded, and similar and recurrent themes were clustered in main categories. Also incorporated were relevant data from a research project which studied the impact of respiratory isolation on patients.[19]

BENEFITS

- Integrated health and social care is perceived as supportive to personal needs (social, cultural and environmental).
- Integrated HIV and TB service provision is valued as important, promoting continuity, consistency and co-ordination of care.
- Family-centred tuberculosis care promotes adherence with follow-up appointments and treatment, minimising disruption of daily routine and/or family lives.
- Flexible appointment system enhances adherence to follow-up appointments and treatment, minimising disruption of personal/family lives.
- Fast-track access/service reduces anxiety, enabling rapid access to care.
- Case Management is valued for its continuity, consistency and co-ordination of care in hospital, out-patient and community settings.
- Regular follow-up promotes sustained support and adherence to treatment.
- Regular follow-up promotes the development of a trusting patient-carer relationship/dynamics.
- TB Nurses are perceived as a constant and reliable source of information, guidance and encouragement.

LIMITATIONS

- Long waiting time for nursing consultation during walk-in clinics, on occasion.
- Long waiting time for consultation with TB physician at booked appointments, on occasion.
- Separate medical follow-up appointments for parents and children.
- No evening or weekend appointments.
- Long waiting time in pharmacy, at times.
- Prescriptions dispensed incompletely by Pharmacy, at times, resulting in additional travel costs to collect medication, confusion and/or adherence failure.
- Delays, occasionally, in obtaining adherence aids, such as a Dosett box or Medidos system (due to local hospital Pharmacy policy, coupled with staff shortage), affecting treatment adherence.
- Required payment of TB medication, but supplied free of charge if co-infected with HIV (local hospital policy).
- Limited treatment enablers and incentives.
- Limited adherence support on an outreach-basis.
- No routine contact screening on an outreach-basis.
- No rapid access to interpreters.
- No rapid referral/access to social workers, benefits advisors or housing.
- Health Promotion material available only in English and in written format.

FEEDBACK FROM HEALTH/SOCIAL PROVIDERS: NURSE-LED SERVICE & CASE MANAGEMENT

EVALUATION METHOD

Informal feedback, comments made and views expressed by other health and social providers, were recorded, similar and recurrent themes clustered in main categories. Also incorporated is relevant data from a research project which studied the impact of respiratory isolation on patients.[19]

- **BENEFITS**
- Integrated health and social care across medical specialities are valued.
- Rapid response and fast-track access/service is valued.
- Specialist skills and knowledge of the TB CNS team are valued – for consultancy, support and guidance.
- Case Management aids discharge planning – sustained patient-focused involvement by the TB CNS from the moment treatment is to be commenced.
- Case Management promotes co-ordination, consistency and continuity – across inpatient, outpatient and community settings.
- The TB nursing team is regarded as an important source of clinical guidance and decision making.
- Improved patient care – continuity and consistency, across disciplines and sectors.
- Improved tuberculosis control – across disciplines and sectors.
- Awareness of issues relating to TB treatment, management and control – across disciplines and sectors.
- Participants from across hospital specialities/disciplines noted regular teaching sessions as important for increased understanding and change in practice in order to improve care and disease control.
- The TB Symposia were highly evaluated and recommended by delegates as catalysts for increased understanding and change in practice, especially presentations delivered by individuals with personal experience of tuberculosis treatment.

- **LIMITATIONS**
- No specific new entrant screening clinic.
- No general BCG vaccination Clinic (available only for those identified as TB contacts or during new entrant screening).
- Prescriptions dispensed incompletely by Pharmacy, at times, resulting in confusion / adherence failure.
- Required payment of TB medication, but free of charge if co-infected with HIV (local hospital policy).
- Limited treatment enablers and incentives.
- Limited adherence support on an outreach-basis.
- No permanent Outreach Workers or routine contact screening on an outreach-basis.
- No community-based TB screening programme.
- No rapid referral/access to social workers, benefits advisors or housing.
- No rapid access to interpreters. Health Promotion material available only in English and in written format.
- No ongoing teaching programmes in the community.
- Cascade of rising workload for other providers without additional/specialist funding, e.g. Pharmacy (increased prescriptions, demand for rapid availability of adherence aids, etc.); Microbiology (increased specimens, demand for rapid availability of culture identification and sensitivities); Paediatric, Chest and HIV Departments (increased referrals, need for rapid medical intervention, etc.).
- Therapy Support Worker position not filled, increasing nursing workload.
- Lack of research component.

LIMITATIONS

Despite significant improvements in service organisation, delivery and treatment outcome several central limitations prevail, in addition to those already highlighted, the central theme being too few resources and insufficient investment in tuberculosis control.

EVALUATION AND RESEARCH

As a result of the lack of financial investment in tuberculosis control, coupled with its novelty in the UK, there is currently limited analysed data (quantitative and qualitative) of the effectiveness of this Nurse-led programme. Nevertheless, key achievements in service organisation and delivery [see pages 31-32], feedback from patients [see page 33] and health/social providers [see page 34], and the available quantitative data as previously discussed, are extremely encouraging and since the introduction of this Nurse-led Service the quality of gathered information has improved significantly. Formal research studies should be commissioned to assess the qualitative and quantitative impact on both individual and public health of a Nurse-led Model with Case Management approach.

STRATEGIC PLANNING

A general lack of strategic vision and planning, both within and between hospital and community settings, contributes to the ongoing dearth of resources and insufficient investment in tuberculosis control. It also adds to a common lack of appreciation of the crucial importance of fully integrated TB service provision. Consequently, there is no formally agreed service specification between hospital, community and Public Health sectors, with resulting confusion regarding sectoral and service responsibilities, accountabilities and boundaries.

ROLE CLARITY

Multisectoral strategic and service specification planning would also help to clarify and further strengthen the individual responsibilities and accountabilities of key players, such as the differing but complementing roles of the TB Service Manager and Trust Lead Physician in service development, and that of the local CCDC and the TB CNS team in investigating potential sites of cross-infections and outbreaks in the community.

SERVICE PROVISION

The scope and effectiveness of service provision are severely restricted by the absence of specialist funding, resulting in a lack of clinical / social support and expertise and a frequent change of staff. Another attributable factor is the ongoing split between the acute and community sectors regarding shared responsibilities/goals for patient care and funding for specialist service provision. The lack of resources has a direct affect on the availability of and access to care. For example (1) adherence management strategies are predominantly hospital rather than outreach/community-based, therefore failing to respond to identified patient needs, and (2) innovative interventions are required to respond appropriately and effectively to the characteristics of the local population groups, such as specific health / social needs associated with HIV / TB co-infection and transient inner city populations.

Also, a trial period identified the need for a specific screening clinic for new entrants, by booked appointment. This allowed for prior assessment and response to individual linguistic needs and arrangement for interpreter support. However, lack of financial investment resulted in an appointment waiting time of over six months, which is highly inappropriate for a local transient population and the level of available resources. Consequently, resources had to be focused on effective management of TB symptomatic patients and those diagnosed with tuberculosis, instead of routine screening. Therefore, until additional funding can be secured, the provision of a specialist new entrant screening clinic is no longer feasible. Screening of new entrants is now restricted to walk-in clinics, resulting in low uptake and inability to respond to cultural and linguistic needs.

ADHERENCE MANAGEMENT
The ability of nurses to implement flexible, appropriate and acceptable programmes and to visit those who fail to attend appointments is limited by staffing levels. Due to a lack of financial resources no incentives or enablers can be offered to patients, except assistance with travel costs for those residing locally. Also, the statutory payment of anti-TB medication,[27] unless exempted, can be a significant barrier to adherence.

The availability, provision and acceptance of adherence aids and strategies are also dependent on the level of resources, staffing levels and policies of partnering disciplines. For example, organisational barriers could be created through delays, inconvenience and disruption caused by the temporary unavailability of certain drugs, such as elixir and combination tablets; incomplete dispensing of prescriptions; delayed dispensing of adherence aids; and rigid policies regarding responsibility for the re-filling and ongoing management of adherence aids.

EDUCATION & TRAINING
Due to extremely limited resources, financial and specialist staff, and a lack of strategic investment in tuberculosis control, it is not possible to implement a sustained educational/training programme at hospital, primary care or community levels.

HEALTH PROMOTION
There is an existing need for a range of comprehensive information, targeted at specific vulnerable populations, health and social care professionals and for the public in general. In addition, due to lack of funding, available health promotion materials do not reflect the cultural and linguistic diversity of the patient/population groups. They are available only in English and in written format.

SOCIAL AND INTERPRETER SERVICES
Although referrals are made to social workers and interpreters, they are not an integrated part of the service and there is no rapid access, resulting in delayed interventions, which affects the distribution of disease, treatment outcome and access to health and healthcare in general.

OUTREACH
Community-based and outreach service provision is restricted by staffing levels and exacerbated by the 'acute and community sector divide'. Further, inner city transport and traffic problems make it difficult and time consuming for staff to reach patients within a large geographical urban area.

ADMIN AND SECRETARIAL SUPPORT
Due to insufficient funding, no such support is available for the TB CNS team. Consequently, Case Managers are responsible for their own administrative duties including the typing of all correspondence, thus impeding role responsibilities, including clinical activities, adherence management and actual service provision.

LEVEL OF NURSES
As previously discussed due to limited resources and lack of financial investment in tuberculosis control Case Managers have to take on responsibility for an over-heavy caseload, with possible negative implications for individualised patient-focused care, disease control and other duties such as adherence support and education. ●

RECOMMENDATIONS

There is a pressing need to review, rejuvenate and reconstruct service provision for effective tuberculosis control, a process which may require consideration of the following issues:

FUNDING

New structures encouraging joint-funding are crucial. A three-pronged approach, uniting key players within the Hospital, Community and Public Health sectors may be more powerful as a combined force in negotiations than a segregated approach. Posts and service activities could be funded from various sectors and/or specialities, but should however, be managed centrally by the TB Service to encourage seamless service provision – continuity, co-ordination and consistency. The actual source and base of funding are not as significant as determinants of effective tuberculosis control as the scope and cross-sectoral freedom of practice.

Public Health should play a stronger role in facilitating the securing of specialist funding for improved service provision, audit/evaluation and ongoing development.

There should be strategic planning and review of the impact of improved tuberculosis service provision on the workload of other specialities/disciplines, including the need for more resources, such as specialist nurses, physicians, isolation and diagnostic facilities, and other support workers.

CENTRALITY

Hospital-based TB Services may be more effective in seamless service provision if not managerially bound to a specific medical speciality, but clinically still responsible to the Trust Lead Physician. This should equip TB CNSs with further 'neutrality' enabling them to cross boundaries without creating interdepartmental tensions. The managerial structure and seamless practice of Infection Control Teams might serve as a helpful example in consideration of a framework for a central TB nursing team.

ROLE CLARIFICATION

The role of the nominated Trust Lead TB Physician needs to be formalised with defined responsibility and accountability.

The specific and complementary role responsibilities and accountabilities of the TB Service Manager, TB CNSs and Trust Lead Physician must be clearly outlined.

The specific and differing responsibility and accountability in terms of service provision, development and management of different nursing grades must be clearly identified.

Service specification needs to be agreed jointly between managerial/executive levels at Hospital, Community and Public Health sector to clarify actual, expected and funded level of service provision, responsibility and accountability.

LEVEL OF NURSES

The British Thoracic Society guidelines recommend that for every 50 patients notified with tuberculosis per year, a minimum of one TB nurse specialist with full clerical support should be appointed.[28] This ratio has been criticised as wholly inadequate for London and effective Case Management.[12,21] As previously discussed, in order to provide safely and effectively individualised patient-focused tuberculosis care and control, Case Management experience at St. Mary's Hospital would suggest a minimum of one nurse per caseload of twenty-five to thirty patients if the Case Manager has full admin and secretarial support and is not routinely responsible for administering DOT/DOPT. Also, any proposed nurse-to-patient ratio must be calculated according to the actual and projected size of the caseload, not only on the number of notifications. Any proposals must take into consideration the number of patients on full anti-TB treatment and chemoprophylaxis. In addition if nursing strategies for tuberculosis care and control are to be implemented successfully, the total number of individuals under investigation for possible infection/disease must also be included in any projections - also, the time for additional activities such as health promotion and education. However, if a team of 'support workers' could assume responsibilities for admin and secretarial input plus activities such as administering DOT/DOPT and tracing non-attendees, then there would be the potential for a reviewed nurse-patient ratio.

However, in spite of strong concerns raised by TB Nurses throughout London, the NHS Executive in their recent recommendations for improving tuberculosis control recommends that each sector should achieve initially a level of one nurse for 50 notifications, progressing to one nurse for 40 notifications by April 2002.[21] This statement raises concerns for effective tuberculosis control because of the possibility that at Management and Commissioner levels these guidelines could be utilised as a yardstick, irrespective of local population or service requirements. Further, key fund holders tend to focus exclusively on local notification statistics, failing to acknowledge and account for the impact on resources of patients resident outside but managed by the local TB Service. Recommendations for funding tend to be apportioned according to the nurse-patient ratio based on local notifications only. In addition, the current proposed levels for TB Nurses do not acknowledge the additional nursing input and resources required for the effective management of patients co-infected with HIV.[12] These recommendations once again fully fail to endorse the key role of nursing in effective tuberculosis control because a formal study of the appropriately recommended staffing levels has not yet been conducted.

TB CNS ROLE DEVELOPMENT

There should be ongoing development of the role of the TB Nurse as specialist practitioner in tuberculosis care and control with consideration of the role of the TB Consultant Nurse.[29]

Attention is required to the advancement of professional development opportunities and career prospects for the specialist TB Nurse. For example, consideration of role development as a Public Health Nurse Specialist in TB control, thereby promoting the widening of skills, expertise and career opportunities. This might be a marketing incentive to encourage nurses into this field of healthcare, aiding the lack of nurses in particular, and problems associated with recruiting TB nurses.

Payment of a 'TB allowance', in line with agreed entitlements for nurses in certain areas, such as those working in HIV-related specialities, could serve as further incentives for recruitment and retention.

ADHERENCE MANAGEMENT STRATEGIES

There should be ongoing development and evaluation of various adherence management strategies, with emphasis on the elimination of organisational/structural barriers to adherence.[30]

Community-based workers who are unable to assist with the provision of adherence support/ monitoring should be requested to confirm this in writing, not to be used as a punitive tool but as evidence for the appropriate need for specialist funding for sustained adherence strategies, co-ordinated and managed by the TB Service.

Availability of adherence support on an outreach-basis, strategies funded jointly across sectors but co-ordinated and managed by the TB Service is essential. For example, consideration for the employment of Therapy Support Workers at Health Care Assistant or equivalent level, working across hospital and community settings similar to the Public Health Advisors in New York City.[14]

There should be increased involvement of patients and community groups with experience of tuberculosis in service development, delivery, evaluation and advocacy work.[17, 31]

PEOPLE/COMMUNITY-FOCUSED SERVICE DEVELOPMENT

Implementation of satellite programmes for TB screening and general nursing follow-up including adherence management should be considered. They should be situated within a geographical area promoting easy access and uptake of services by disadvantaged and 'at risk' communities, such as refugees, asylum seekers and those resident in temporary accommodation. Such programmes should be funded jointly across sectors and developed in partnership with local community organisations, such as Primary Care Groups and those serving the respective communities/populations.

Availability and access to standard TB screening should be made available throughout the community. All health providers, such as GP practices, District Nurses and Health Visitors should be trained to offer basic TB screening in line with protocol, agreed jointly between the TB Service, Public Health and respective organisations. Referrals to the local TB Service should be necessary only when abnormalities are detected, such as the presence of TB symptoms or abnormal screening results. This should increase uptake of screening and decrease the workload caused by routine screening within the TB Service.

The minimisation in disruption of people's lives, particularly those of families, should be a central focus of service development to increase availability, access and uptake. For example a strategy for consideration is the provision of a Family TB Clinic, incorporating care for both parents and children.

There should be an opening-up and a creation of career opportunities for the non-medically trained and lay people to work in tuberculosis control. Employees should be recruited to reflect the socio-cultural diversities of the local patient population. Such a strategy should help to overcome certain structural barriers such as linguistic differences, thereby increasing the level of service provision and uptake without adding to the workload of the TB CNS team, who are already under pressure, over-stretched and under staffed. This could be a cost saving strategy through improved completion rates, prevention of relapse and drug resistance, and reduced spread of infection.

Instead of a focus predominantly on directly observed therapy as a method to improve rates of treatment completion, careful consideration should be given to other factors which may enhance treatment, such as heightened professional and public awareness of tuberculosis; increased service availability, access and uptake; clinical expertise, leadership and service management; improved care provision – consistency, co-ordination and continuity of care; sustained patient support and encouragement; and critical reflection on possible organisational barriers to effective tuberculosis care and control.

A patient satisfaction assessment tool for process and outcome evaluation should be incorporated as an integral component of standard Case Management documentation, allowing systematic evaluation and service user involvement for future service development.

RESEARCH

Formal research to study the appropriately recommended nurse-patient staffing levels according to the local setting should be commissioned.

Formal research studies should be conducted to assess the qualitative and quantitative impact on both individual and public health of a Nurse-led Model with Case Management approach.

There should be analysis of the type and level of overall scope for cost improvements through Nurse-led service provision.

EDUCATION AND AWARENESS RAISING

Educational programmes should be developed aimed at health/social providers and policy makers to increase understanding of the far reaching affects of tuberculosis and to develop skills and expertise for appropriate public health responses.

Targeted health promotion interventions for heightened public awareness of the problem should be commissioned, creating desired opportunities for collaboration across sectors, e.g. between TB Services, service users/patients, Health Promotion Units/Departments and community-based organisations serving local communities.

TB TREATMENT OUTCOMES

Careful consideration should be given to appropriate definitions of treatment outcome categories. Some of the current definitions are too limited with the possibility of negative reflection on completion outcomes.[32] For example, it seems these categories penalise the service providers in terms of overall treatment completion rates by having to include in their final calculations those patients categorised under 'transferred out' even if such transfers were facilitated with full support and continuation of therapy, nationally or internationally. Subsequently, should treatment fail or no outcome information obtained, the initial treatment centre remains at fault. Similar penalties seem to be incurred when a patient is 'still on treatment', or has 'died', even if the death is incidental. Stronger emphasis on the total number categorised as 'failure', 'loss to follow-up' and 'unknown' might perhaps reveal results that are more accurate in terms of actual successes, improvements and treatment achievements.

Also, there is a need for the development of suitable definitions for chemoprophylaxis treament outcome categories. This should apply pressure to the notion that sustained patient support, adherence and outcome monitoring should be of equal importance.

ETHICAL FRAMEWORK

In light of diverse multi-cultural patient / population groups, there is an existing Importance to work with them, and with community organisations representing and serving them, to develop an appropriate ethical framework for TB control in order to ensure cross-cultural sensitivity and acceptability. ⬤

CONCLUSION

In London, the role of the TB Nurse and actual service provision varies according to geographical setting. Services are unable to respond sufficiently to the growing incidence of tuberculosis, highlighting the need for change.[3,10,21] These difficulties are attributed to fragmentation caused by the current organisational structures, too few resources and too little investment in tuberculosis control. With the multiplicity and complexity of the challenges associated with the ongoing rise of tuberculosis, programmes for effective control require innovative planning and evaluation, responding to local health and population needs.

The experience at St. Mary's Hospital demonstrates the positive changes produced by the implementation of a Nurse-led model with a Case Management approach, and the value of Case Management models also has been noted in the USA.[14,15,33-36] Within such a framework of practice the TB CNS, as Case Manager, is the interface for fully integrated individualised patient care and effective tuberculosis control, functioning across traditional barriers such as those between different medical specialities and between hospital and community settings. This approach ensures continuity of care, sustains a consistent, co-ordinated and supportive approach and fosters adherence to treatment, promoting both individual and public health to enhance appropriate service delivery.

Some aspects of improvement were achieved simply through the reorganisation of the structure of service provision and the development of the role of the TB CNS, which required minimal financial investment. However, the overall success of such a model demands sustained financial investment and ongoing support and commitment from key players. Restructuring the organisation and commissioning of Tuberculosis Services in London are urgently needed in order to decrease fragmentation, increase co-ordination and improve standards of service delivery. Central productive steps would include consideration of the essential role of the TB nurse and modernisation of conventional control programmes which would in turn lead to emphasis on the implementation of a 'Nurse-led' Tuberculosis Service with a Case Management approach. In addition, thought must be given to the inclusion in tuberculosis care and control of non-medically trained and lay people.

It is not suggested that this model is the best framework for the provision of fully integrated tuberculosis care and control, but its performance at St. Mary's demonstrates its feasibility. In some settings at least such a model is workable and with additional resources may be highly effective towards successful tuberculosis control in London.

There is an urgent need to view the control of TB within a broader, more structurally contextualised perspective. Strategists must examine the disease and treatment from the perspective of the individual at local population level, examining critically the structural influences which pattern inequalities and shape disease distribution and treatment outcomes.

We need a modern formula for the establishment of a 'horizontal-population-focused' method for service development, demanding community, transdisciplinary and cross-sectoral collaboration for integrated needs assessment. Policy and service planning must be formulated in partnership with patients / population groups and with community organizations representing and serving them, responding to contextual structural barriers (e.g. cultural, political, economical and organizational determinants) influencing the spread and control of tuberculosis in order to guide socio-culturally sensitive, acceptable and appropriate programmatic responses.

There is also an urgency to analyse critically, rigorously and systematically the ethical foundations and the knowledge, values and beliefs that underpin our professional, personal and social actions, and also inform policy making and public health responses, so that the protection of the public does not result in the persecution of the individual. This is the fundamental challenge of providing care for infectious patients while protecting society at large.

Advocacy of traditional disease control strategies, without critical and sustained attention to structural determination and structural inequalities will fuel the spread of tuberculosis, reinforcing instead of redressing 'structural violence'.[38] There is need for a modern public health paradigm in the treatment of TB. Reductionism must be replaced with integration. A syncretic approach would be an advantageous progression, combining community-focused responses with medicine. This could create a dynamic, critical and structuralist formula which would not segregate the individual, the disease and methods for control from their contextual cultural, socio-political and organizational context. Integrated programmatic responses which focus attention on the complex relationship between contextual structural forces, biological factors and individual ability toward disease prevention can lead to the innovative strategies we so desperately need. ▇

DIAGRAMS & TABLES

DIAGRAM 1.0 NURSE-LED SERVICE: TUBERCULOSIS CARE & CONTROL

Within a Nurse-led Service, the TB CNS is the pivot for effective individualised tuberculosis care and disease control across disciplines and sectors, safeguarding both individual and public health.

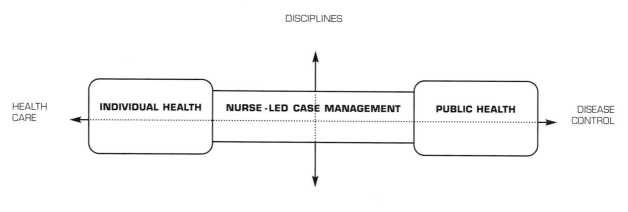

DIAGRAM 2.0 TB CONTROL: NURSE-LED MODEL WITH CASE MANAGEMENT

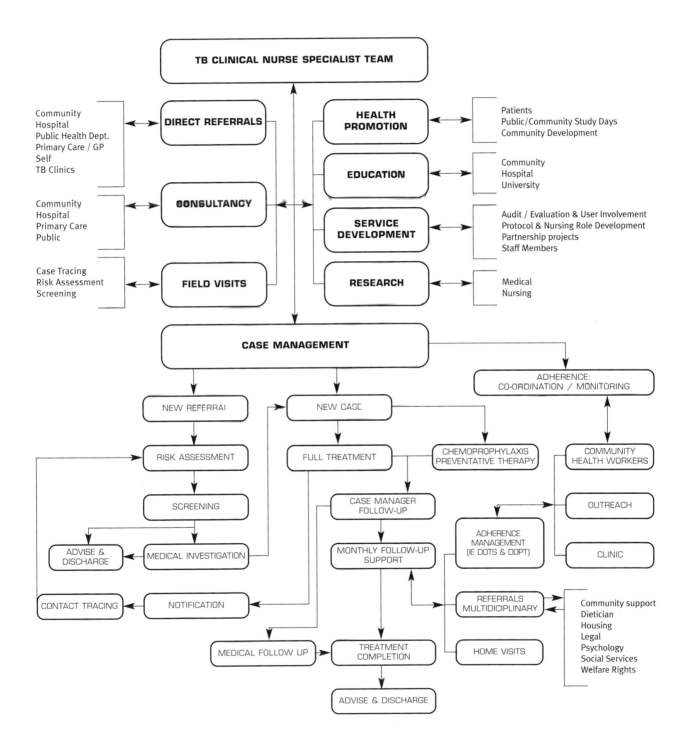

DIAGRAM 3.0 TEAM STRUCTURE

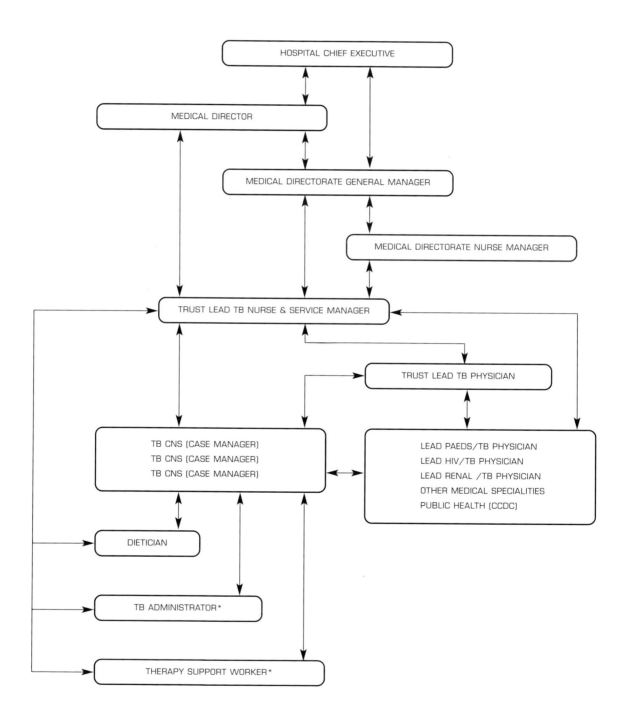

KEYS:

* Positions to be created / appointed.

TABLE 1.0 STATISTICS: TB SERVICE, ST. MARY'S HOSPITAL

YEAR	NOTIFICATIONS	CHEMOPROPHYLAXIS	TOTAL THERAPY CASELOAD
1992	56	NOT RECORDED	56
1993	77	22 (JULY-DECEMBER)	99
1994	103	29	132
1995	119	28	147
1996	177[A]	39	216
1997	149	40	189
1998	159	47	206
1999	156[B]	62 [B]	218 [B]

DEFINITIONS:

A. Includes HIV co-infected patients who were on treatment during 1995 but TB Service not informed, subsequently traced and notified retrospectively by the HIV/TB CNS in 1996.

B. Reduced screening and referrals due to national shortage of PPD for Heaf/Mantoux Testing .

TABLE 2.0 TREATMENT OUTCOMES: ACTIVE TUBERCULOSIS

	JAN-DEC'97H	JAN-DEC'98	JAN-DEC'99
NO. OF NOTIFICATIONS DURING THIS PERIOD	149 / 22 HIV+	159	156
TREATMENT COMPLETIONA	16 HIV+	121	117
STILL ON TREATMENT	NIL HIV+	NIL	3
TREATMENT FAILURE	NIL HIV+	NIL	NIL
DEATH	2 HIV+	9	5
TRANSFERRED OUTB	2 HIV+	12	20
LOST TO FOLLOW-UP	NIL HIV+	4 (X3 IN ONE FAMILY)	1
UNKNOWNC	NIL HIV+	NIL	NIL
DENOTIFIED	2 HIV+	13	10
TREATMENT COMPLETION RATE (%)D	16/16 = 100% HIV+	121/125 = 97%	117/118 = 99%
TREATMENT COMPLETION RATE (%)E	16/18 = 89% HIV+	121/134 = 90%	117/123 = 95%
KNOWN HIV-COINFECTED (%)F	22/149 = 15%	20/159 = 13%	9/156 = 6%
PAEDIATRIC CASES (%)	16/149 = 11%	28/159 = 18%	34/156 = 22%
PATIENTS RESIDENT OUTSIDE LOCAL HA (%)G	16/22 = 73% HIV+	62/159 = 39%	45/156 = 29%

DEFINITION OF CATEGORIES: [BASED ON THE TB TREATMENT OUTCOME CATEGORIES FOR LONDON, PHLS, CDSC LONDON].[32]

A. All patients: case managed, completed full course of therapy, officially discharged and recorded in TB documentation.
B. All patients: case managed, care actively transferred to another centre, nationally or abroad, with no further involvement or outcome evaluation.
C. All patients: no information available about the outcome of the patient due to missing notes or outcome data not collected/recorded.
D. All patients: excluding total numbers of those categorised under 'still on treatment', 'death', 'transferred out' and 'denotified'.
E. All patients: excluding total numbers of those categorised under 'still on treatment', 'transferred out' and 'denotification'.
F. All patients: confirmed diagnosis of co-infection with HIV.
G. All patients: approximate percentage not resident in local HA, out of the total number of notifications.
H. Incomplete documentation or unavailable records. Full records available only of patients co-infected with HIV.

TABLE 3.0 TREATMENT OUTCOMES: CHEMOPROPHYLAXIS FOR TUBERCULOSIS

	JAN-DEC'97H	JAN-DEC'98	JAN-DEC'99
NO. OF CASES DURING THIS PERIOD	40 / 28 HIV+	47	62
TREATMENT COMPLETION[A]	20 HIV+	43	54
STILL ON TREATMENT	NIL HIV+	NIL	NIL
DEATH	NIL HIV+	NIL	1
TRANSFERRED OUT[B]	3 HIV+	2	2
LOST TO FOLLOW-UP	1 HIV+	1	NIL
TREATMENT STOPPED: DRUG INTOLERANCE	2 HIV+	1	2
TREATMENT STOPPED: POOR ADHERENCE	1 HIV+	NIL	NIL
TREATMENT STOPPED: INDEX CASE NOT TB	NIL HIV+	NIL	3
PATIENT DID NOT COMMENCE, THEN DECLINED	1 HIV+	NIL	NIL
TREATMENT COMPLETION RATE (%)[C]	20/21 = 95% HIV+	43/44 = 98%	54/54= 100%
TREATMENT COMPLETION RATE (%)[D]	20/21 = 95% HIV+	43/44 = 98%	54/55= 98%
KNOWN HIV-COINFECTED (%)[E]	28/40 = 70% HIV+	22/47 = 47%	15/62 = 24%
PAEDIATRIC CASES (%)	12/40 = 30%	23/47 = 49%	42/62 = 68%
PATIENTS RESIDENT OUTSIDE LOCAL HA (%)[F]	14/28 = 50% HIV+	19/47 = 40%	22/62 = 35%
UNKNOWN[G]	NIL HIV+	NIL	NIL

DEFINITION OF CATEGORIES: [BASED ON THE TB TREATMENT OUTCOME CATEGORIES FOR LONDON, PHLS, CDSC LONDON].[32]

A. All patients: case managed, completed full course of chemoprophylaxis, officially discharged and recorded in TB documentation.
B. All patients: case managed, care actively transferred to another centre, nationally or abroad, with no further involvement or outcome evaluation.
C. Excluding total numbers of those categorised under 'still on treatment', 'death', 'transferred out' and 'treatment stopped', and 'patient did not commence'.
D. Excluding total numbers of those categorised under 'still on treatment', 'transferred out' and 'treatment stopped', and 'patient did not commence'.
E. All patients: confirmed diagnosis of co-infection with HIV.
F. All patients: approximate percentage not resident in local HA, out of the total number of notifications.
G. All patients: no information available about the outcome of the patient due to missing notes or outcome data not collected/recorded.
H. Incomplete documentation or unavailable records. Full records available only of patients co-infected with HIV.

REFERENCES

1   Public Health Laboratory Service Communicable Disease Surveillance Centre (2001) *Tuberculosis (all forms) Notifications. Annual Totals England & Wales;* 1982-1999 Public Health Laboratory Service Communicable Disease Surveillance Centre, UK

2   Public Health Laboratory Service Communicable Disease Surveillance Centre (2000) *UK Mycobacterial Resistance Network (Mycobnet)* Public Health Laboratory Service Communicable Disease Surveillance Centre, UK.

3   NHS Executive (1998) *Tuberculosis control in London: the need for change.* NHS Executive, London.

4   Communicable Disease Report (1995) Outbreak of hospital acquired multidrug-resistant tuberculosis. *CDR Weekly* 5(34), 161.

5   Communicable Disease Report (1996) Multidrug resistant tuberculosis in a London hospital. *CDR Weekly* 6(24), 205.

6   Project Megapoles (1999) *Health in Europe's capitals* European Commission.

7   London Research Centre (1999) *Projected all resident population* Public Health Department, Kensington, Chelsea & Westminster Health Authority, London.

8   Kensington, Chelsea and Westminster Health Authority (1999) *The health of refugees* HA(99)2.1 Kensington, Chelsea & Westminster Health Authority, London.

9   Department of Health (1998) *Independent inquiry into inequalities in health report 1998* The Stationery Office, London.

10 Marais F. (2000) Disease prevention: lung haul *Health Service Journal* June, 31.

11 Pym A.S., Churchill D.R., Coker R.J. & Gleissberg V. (1995) Reasons for increased incidence of tuberculosis *British Medical Journal* 311, 570.

12 Marais F. (1998) Progress towards controlling HIV-associated TB upsurge. *Nursing Times* 94(11), 54-55.

13 New Jersey Medical School National Tuberculosis Center (1997) Nurse Case Management and its application to the treatment of patients with tuberculosis. *Education and Training Calendar,* January – December 1997. National Tuberculosis Center, New Jersey Medical School, Newark.

14 Dorsinville M.S. (1998) Case Management of tuberculosis in New York City. *International Journal of Tuberculosis and Lung Disease* 2(9), S46-S52.

15 Berroa J. (1998) Case Management: a nursing point of view. *International Journal of Tuberculosis and Lung Disease* 2(9), S53-S56.

16 Beattie A. (1991) Knowledge and control in health promotion: a test case for social policy and social theory. In: *The sociology of the Health Service* (Gabe J., Calnan M. & Bury M.) Routledge, London.

17 El-Sadr W., Medard F. & Dickerson M. (1995) The Harlem Family Model: a unique approach to the treatment of tuberculosis. *Journal of Public Health Management Practice* 1(4), 48-51.

18 Marshall B.G., Mitchell D.M., Shaw R.J., Marais F., Watkins R.M. & Coker R.J. (1999) HIV and tuberculosis co-infection in an inner London hospital: a prospective anonymised seroprevalence study. *Journal of Infection* 38, 162-166.

19 Marais F. (1999) The impact of the experience of respiratory isolation on the well-being of individuals with tuberculosis: scope for health promotion strategies, South Bank University, London (unpublished).

20 British Thoracic Society (1998) Chemotherapy and management of tuberculosis in the United Kingdom: recommendations 1998. Joint Tuberculosis Committee of the British Thoracic Society *Thorax* 53, 536-548.

21 NHS Executive (2000) *Improving TB control in London* NHS Executive, London.

22 Derbyshire J.H. (1995) Tuberculosis: old reasons for a new increase. *British Medical Journal* 310, 954-5.

23 Balogun M.A., Wall P.G. & Noone A. (1996) Undernotification of tuberculosis in patients with AIDS. *International Journal of STD & AIDS* 7, 58-60.

24 Calden G., Lewis W.C. & Thurston J.R. (1956) The patient looks at tuberculosis. In: Sparer P.(ed) *Personality, stress and tuberculosis* International University Press, New York; 275-299.

25 Kelly-Rossini L., Perlman D.C. & Mason D.J. (1996) The experience of respiratory isolation for HIV-infected persons with tuberculosis *Journal of the Association of Nurses in AIDS Care* 7(1), 29-36.

26 Schulte J.M., Nolt B.J., Williams R.L., Spinks C.L. & Hellsten J.J. (1998) Violence and threats of violence experienced by public health field-workers *Journal of the American Medical Association* 280(5), 439-442.

27 Department of Health (1998) *The drug tariff* 1998 Department of Health, UK.

28 British Thoracic Society (2000) Control and prevention of tuberculosis in the United Kingdom: Code of Practice 2000. Joint Tuberculosis Committee of the British Thoracic Society *Thorax* 55, 887-901.

29 NHS Executive (1999) *Nurse, midwife and health visitor consultants: establishing posts and making appointments* HSC 199/217 NHS Executive, London.

30 Marais F. (2001) Adherence to therapy: Carrot or Stick? Reflections on lessons in TB control *Culture, Health & Sexuality* (submitted).

31 Blinkhoff P., Bukanga E., Syamalevwe B. & Williams G. (1999) *Under the Mupundu tree: volunteers in home care for people with HIV/AIDS and TB in Zambia's Copperbelt.* Strategies for Hope Series No.14, ACTIONAID, UK. TALC, UK.

32 Public Health Laboratory Service Communicable Disease Surveillance Centre (2000) *Tuberculosis treatment outcome categories for London* Public Health Laboratory Service Communicable Disease Surveillance Centre, UK.

33 Verbal communication with Pamela Kellner, Director for Program Development, Bureau of Tuberculosis Control, The City of New York, Department of Health, New York; May 1997 & November 2000.

34 Verbal communication with Suzanne Banda, Public Health Nurse, Training Specialist, Francis J. Curry, National Tuberculosis Centre, San Francisco; November 2000.

35 Verbal communication with Dr L. Masae Kawamura, Director, TB Control Division, Department of Public Health, San Francisco, USA; November 2000.

36 Moser K.S. (2000) *Policy and Procedures: Public Health Nurse Case Manager* Tuberculosis Control, San Diego County Health and Human Services Agency, San Diego, USA.

37 North West London Sector (2000) *Plan for Tuberculosis Control* NHS Executive, London.

38 Farmer P. (1999) *Infections and inequalities: the modern plagues* University of California Press, USA.

APPENDIX 1.0

JOB DESCRIPTION: TB CLINICAL NURSE SPECIALIST (GRADES F & G)

CLINICAL NURSE SPECIALIST: TB JOB DESCRIPTION

JOB TITLE: Clinical Nurse Specialist
GRADE: F
LOCATION: TB Service

LINE RELATIONSHIP

MANAGERIALLY ACCOUNTABLE TO: Manager & Lead Nurse
PROFESSIONALLY ACCOUNTABLE TO: Director of Nursing
CLINICALLY RESPONSIBLE TO: Lead Physician

JOB SUMMARY

This post plays a central role in the diagnosis and treatment of individuals with tuberculosis - adults and children, including those co-infected with HIV - across all Directorates and Departments within the Trust.

The post holder, therefore, works within a multidisciplinary team and is responsible for the assessment of care needs, the development, implementation and evaluation of programmes of care. The post holder will provide specialist advice to, and liaise with, a variety of internal departments and other external statutory and non-statutory services.

RESPONSIBILITIES

CLINICAL:

1. To screen, treat and manage patients according to agreed protocols under the supervision of the Manager & Lead Nurse and the Lead Physician.

2. To evaluate and update clinical protocols and policies for the diagnosis, treatment and management of tuberculosis in conjunction with the Manager & Lead Nurse and the Lead Physician.

3. To implement monitoring and evaluation systems for the role of the TB Nurse in conjunction with the Manager & Lead Nurse and the Lead Physician.

4. To monitor the standards of nursing practice through assessment, evaluation and audit in conjunction with the Manager & Lead Nurse.

5. To assist with the provision of nurse-led TB Clinics in line with agreed protocols and under supervision.

6. To refer patients/clients directly to other specialist professions.

7. To select, carry out and interpret the results of specific tests relating to TB and HIV; e.g. Heaf Test, Mantoux Test, Pre/Post test HIV counselling, blood tests, Recall Antigen Test and Ishihara's test for colour-blindness; and making any necessary referrals.

8. To manage and monitor all monthly TB repeat prescriptions in line with agreed protocols.

9. To identify and keep a record of all cases of tuberculosis, in collaboration with district clinicians, the Department of Microbiology and the Public Health notification system. This constitutes keeping the TB register.

10. To provide ongoing support and advice for patients on TB treatment.

11. To make domicilliary visits following patient discharge from hospital to assess living conditions and possible barriers to compliance.

12. To trace and perform domicilliary visits on non-attenders.

13. To liaise with both the Manager & Lead Nurse and Public Health Consultant with regard to the management of specific complex cases.

14. To investigate cases/outbreaks of MTB - risk assessment, contact tracing and screening - within Westminster Health Authority as identified by the Public Health Consultant and under the supervision of the Manager & Lead Nurse.

15. To liaise with the Public Health Consultant with regard to the epidemiology of tuberculosis and the management of specific cases.

16. To provide specialist advice and guidance to nurses, doctors and other staff within the Trust.

17. To provide specialist advice to external agencies concerning TB and HIV.

18. To teach, and when appropriate, supervise other staff and/or students.

MANAGERIAL:

1. To assist the Manager & Lead Nurse in the development, implementation and evaluation of a Trust wide TB Service.

2. To work in a collaborative manner with other agencies in order to co-ordinate the care of patients and to prevent nosocomial spread of TB.

3. To maintain the databases in both the GUM/HIV and Medical Directorates.

4. To carry out any other duties as requested by the Manager & Lead Nurse.

EDUCATIONAL:

1. To undertake and evaluate the provision of TB specialist education within the Trust, and to external agencies, as directed by the Manager & Lead Nurse.

2. To provide telephone information to members of the public and patients.

3. To develop, maintain and update relevant information and health promotion materials on all aspects of TB.

4. To maintain and update personal knowledge of TB associated health issues.

RESEARCH:

1. To initiate and participate in research, projects and surveys, under the direction of the Manager & Lead Nurse and the Lead Physician.

This job description is intended as a basic guide to the scope and responsibilities. It is subject to regular review and amendment as necessary.

CLINICAL NURSE SPECIALIST: TB PERSON SPECIFICATION

JOB TITLE: CLINICAL NURSE SPECIALIST
LOCATION: TB SERVICE
GRADE: F

REQUIREMENTS	ESSENTIAL	DESIRABLE
EDUCATION & TRAINING	RGN Evidence of continuing professional development.	Relevent post registration qualifications. ENB 934/280. ENB 998 or equivalent.
SKILLS	Awareness of issues relating to TB health care. Knowledge of issues relating to communicable disease control. Willingness to undertake further training to enhance scope of practice. Ability to work as an individual within a multi-disciplinary team. Teaching skills in formal and informal settings.	Computer skills - use of Excel and Word.
EXPERIENCE	Able to understand the use of research, evaluation and audit in practice. Able to demonstrate flexibility in clinical situations. Able to communicate with a wide variety of professionals.	Supervision of junior staff/others. Working within outreach, outpatient and or community services.
PERSONAL QUALITIES	Confidential nature. Excellent communicator. Able to demonstrate an understanding of and commitment to equal opportunities. Experience of managing change.	
OTHER REQUIREMENTS	Reliable work record. Flexible to change.	

CLINICAL NURSE SPECIALIST: TB JOB DESCRIPTION

JOB TITLE: Clinical Nurse Specialist
GRADE: G
LOCATION: TB Service

LINE RELATIONSHIP

MANAGERIALLY ACCOUNTABLE TO: Manager & Lead Nurse: TB Service.
PROFESSIONALLY ACCOUNTABLE TO: Director of Nursing
CLINICALLY RESPONSIBLE TO: Lead Clinician/Consultant: TB

JOB SUMMARY

This post plays a central role in the diagnosis and treatment of individuals with tuberculosis - adults and children, including those co-infected with HIV - and in the development, implementation and evaluation of programmes to control the spread of tuberculosis in both hospital and community settings.

The post holder, therefore, is responsible for the management of his/her own caseload and works within a multidisciplinary team across all Directorates and Departments within the Trust. The post holder will provide specialist advice to, and liaise with, a variety of internal departments and other external statutory and non-statutory services.

RESPONSIBILITIES

CLINICAL:

1. To have continuing responsibility for the assessment of care needs, the development, implementation and evaluation of programmes of care, and the setting of standards of care; under the supervision of the 'Manager & Lead Nurse: TB Service'.

2. To provide nurse-led TB Clinics according to agreed protocols, under the supervision of the 'Manager & Lead Nurse: TB Service' and 'Lead Clinician: TB'.

3. To manage a defined caseload of patients.

4. To screen, treat and manage patients according to agreed protocols, under the supervision of the 'Manager & Lead Nurse: TB Service' and the 'Lead Clinician:TB'.

5. To evaluate and update clinical protocols and policies for the diagnosis, treatment and management of tuberculosis in conjunction with the 'Manager & Lead Nurse: TB Service' and the 'Lead Clinician: TB'.

6. To facilitate the admission and referral of patients to own caseload list.

7. To refer patients/clients direct to other specialist professions and agencies.

8. To select, carry out and interpret the results of specific tests relating to TB and HIV; e.g. Heaf Test, Mantoux Test, Pre/Post test HIV counselling, blood tests, Recall Antigen test and Ishihara's test for colour-blindness; and making any necessary referrals.

9. To manage and monitor the continuation therapy of specific anti-mycobacterium tuberculosis drugs according to agreed protocols.

10. To identify and keep a record of all cases of tuberculosis, in collaboration with district clinicians, the Department

of Microbiology and the Public Health notification system. This constitutes keeping the TB register.

11. To provide ongoing support and advice for patients on TB treatment.

12. To make domiciliary visits following patient discharge from hospital to assess living conditions and possible barriers to compliance.

13. To trace and perform domiciliary visits on non-attendees.

14. To investigate cases/outbreaks of MTB - risk assessment, contact identification, tracing and screening - within Westminster Health Authority as identified by the Public Health Consultant and under the direction of the 'Manager & Lead Nurse: TB Service'.

15. To liaise with the Public Health Consultant with regard to the epidemiology of tuberculosis and the management of specific cases.

16. To provide specialist advice and guidance to nurses, doctors and other staff within the Trust.

17. To provide specialist advice to external agencies concerned with TB and HIV.

18. To teach and, when appropriate, supervise other staff and/or students.

MANAGERIAL:

1. To assist the 'Manager & Lead Nurse: TB Service' in the development, implementation and evaluation of a Trust wide TB Service.

2. To assist the 'Manager & Lead Nurse: TB Service' with the development of clinical protocols for the role of the TB Nurse Specialist and a Nurse-led TB Service.

3. To develop the role of, and act as, 'Link-TB Nurse' for specific Directorates/Departments within the Trust as directed by the 'Manager & Lead Nurse: TB Service'.

4. To refine and implement monitoring and evaluation systems for the role of the TB Nurse Specialist in conjunction with the 'Manager & Lead Nurse: TB Service'.

5. To work in collaborative manner with other agencies in order to co-ordinate the care of patients and to prevent nosocomial spread of TB.

6. To maintain and update databases in both GUM/HIV Directorate and Medical Directorate.

7. To manage the TB Service in the absence of the 'Manager & Lead Nurse: TB Service'.

8. To carry out any other duties as requested by the 'Manager & Lead Nurse: TB Service'.

EDUCATIONAL:

1. To undertake and evaluate the provision of TB specialist education within the Trust, and to external agencies.

2. To provide telephone information to patients and members of the public.

3. To develop, maintain and update relevant information and health promotion materials on all aspects of TB.

4. To maintain and update personal knowledge of TB associated health issues.

RESEARCH:

1. To initiate and participate in research, projects and surveys, under the direction of the 'Manager & Lead Nurse: TB Service' and the 'Lead Clinician: TB'.

This job description is intended as a basic guide to the scope and responsibilities. It is subject to regular review and amendment as necessary.

CLINICAL NURSE SPECIALIST: TB PERSON SPECIFICATION

JOB TITLE: CLINICAL NURSE SPECIALIST
LOCATION: TB SERVICE
GRADE: G

REQUIREMENTS	ESSENTIAL	DESIRABLE
EDUCATION & TRAINING	RGN Relevent post registration qualifications.	ENB R02. ENB 934/280. ENB 998 or equivalent. Relevant nursing / health related degree.
SKILLS	Sound theoretical and practical knowledge of TB management, diagnosis, treatment and control. Knowledge of HIV/infectious diseases care. Willingness to undertake further training to enhance scope of practice. Ability to work as an individual within a multi-disciplinary team. Experience of managing own case-load independently and without supervision. Teaching skills in formal and informal settings. Leadership skills	Knowledge of NHS and wider context Computer skills - use of Excel and Word.
EXPERIENCE	Current clinical experience as TB Nurse/Health Visitor. Experience of the use of research and audit Able to demonstrate flexibility in clinical situations. Able to communicate with a wide variety of professionals. Staff management	Working within protocols Writing Clinical protocols Working within outreach, outpatient and or community services.
PERSONAL QUALITIES	Confidential nature. Excellent communicator. Able to demonstrate an understanding of and commitment to equal opportunities. Experience of managing change. Ability to work autonomously or within a team.	
OTHER REQUIREMENTS	Reliable work record and flexible to change.	

APPENDIX 2.0

JOB DESCRIPTION: THERAPY SUPPORT WORKER

THERAPY SUPPORT WORKER: TB SERVICE JOB DESCRIPTION

JOB TITLE: Therapy Support Worker
GRADE: B (0.48) - 18 hours per week
CONTRACT: 6 months, with possibility of renewal
LOCATION: TB Service

LINE RELATIONSHIP

RESPONSIBLE TO: Manager & Lead Nurse: TB Service
ACCOUNTABLE TO: Medical Directorate Nurse Manager

JOB SUMMARY

This post plays a central role in the treatment of individuals with tuberculosis - adults and children, including those co-infected with HIV - across hospital and community settings.

The post holder will provide care in partnership with the TB Clinical Nurse Specialist Team (Case Managers) and will be responsible for delegated elements of the adherence management care plan of patients.

KEY TASKS AND RESPONSIBILITIES

CLINICAL CARE:

1. To carry out tasks in delivering and supporting direct patient care - delegated from and under the supervision of a TB Clinical Nurse Specialist, or other professionally qualified staff. Able to demonstrate abilities and competencies gained to enable tasks to be delegated from professionally qualified staff.

2. To perform more complex aspects of patient care, some with indirect supervision e.g. venepuncture, taking and recording of observations, doing simple dressings, checking and preparing equipment and preparing patients for treatment by qualified staff - requiring greater knowledge and experience than that demonstrated by Health Care Assistants at Grade A.

3. To assist the TB Clinical Nurse Specialists with the implementation and evaluation of adherence strategies, such as Directly Observed Therapy (DOT), Directly Observed Preventative Therapy (DOPT), Weekly Supervised Therapy (WST) or Monthly Supervised Therapy (MST) - in both hospital and community settings.

4. To demonstrate a courteous and helpful approach to patients and relatives in both hospital and community settings.

5. To demonstrate a high level of interpersonal skills.

6. To deliver Dosett boxes and medicine containers directly to patients in the community - under the direction of the TB Clinical Nurse Specialists and in line with agreed protocols.

7. To provide ongoing support and encouragement to patients in order to ensure effective adherence and completion of treatment - as directed by the TB Clinical Nurse Specialists and in line with agreed protocols.

8. To assess patients for drug side effects and adherence with therapy, and to document observations in the patient's nursing notes - as directed by the TB Clinical Nurse Specialists and in line with agreed protocols.

9. To observe patients taking their medication directly from Dosett boxes and/or medicine containers, and swallowing them - as directed by the TB Clinical Nurse Specialists and in line with agreed protocols.

10. To visit non-attenders at home in order to encourage them to return to the TB Service for assessment

and/or continuation of anti-MTB treatment - as directed by the TB Clinical Nurse Specialists and in line with agreed protocols.

11. To ensure accurate and up-to-date documentation in patients' nursing notes - as directed by the TB Clinical Nurse Specialists.

12. To prioritise own workload in conjunction with the aims and objectives of the TB Service - under the supervision of the TB Clinical Nurse Specialists.

13. To keep clinical areas clean and tidy and maintain a safe and pleasant environment.

14. To assist in the restocking of supplies and maintenance of equipment as directed by a TB Clinical Nurse Specialist.

15. To provide admin & clerical support as directed by a TB Clinical Nurse Specialist.

16. To report immediately untoward incidents and any other relevant information to a TB Clinical Nurse Specialist.

17. To adhere to departmental and Directorate procedures for the use of supplies and equipment in order to promote effective and efficient use of resources.

18. To inform a TB Clinical Nurse Specialist if asked to carry out a task which the Therapy Support Worker does not have the training or capacity to do.

19. To be aware of and adhere to relevant Trust Policies and Procedures - as identified by the TB Clinical Nurse Specialist Team.

TEAM / ORGANISATIONAL

1. To participate, in conjunction with the TB Service team, in the evaluation of strategies and policies for the adherence management of patients with tuberculosis.

2. To participate in the development and evaluation of the role of the Therapy Support Worker in conjunction with the 'Manager & Lead Nurse: TB Service' and the TB Clinical Nurse Specialists.

3. To produce monthly activity reports - as directed by the 'Manager & Lead Nurse: TB Service'.

4. To monitor patient access to adherence strategies/services, record difficulties, and feed back to the TB Clinical Nurse Specialist Team.

5. To collect information for monitoring and planning purposes - as directed by the 'Manager & Lead Nurse: TB Service'.

6. To participate in health promotion/awareness activities - as directed by the TB Clinical Nurse Specialists.

OTHER DUTIES

1. To be actively involved in the development of the TB Service team and committed to the principles of team working.

2. To participate in regular supervision and case discussions.

3. To participate in in-service training and Staff Development Review.

4. To maintain and update personal knowledge of TB associated health issues.

This job description is intended as a basic guide to the scope and responsibilities. The post holder would be required to demonstrate flexibility in order that the TB Service could respond to the changing needs of this population. The job description is subject to regular review and may be altered in the light of changes in full consultation with the post holder.

THERAPY SUPPORT WORKER: TB SERVICE PERSON SPECIFICATION

JOB TITLE: Therapy Support Worker
GRADE: B (0.48) - 18 hours per week
CONTRACT: 6 months, with possibility of renewal
LOCATION: TB Service

REQUIREMENTS	ESSENTIAL	DESIRABLE
EDUCATION & TRAINING	Health / Social care training and/or qualification	Health promotion training Training/education relating to tuberculosis care
EXPERIENCE & KNOWLEDGE	Working within a multi-cultural environment Working with disadvantaged individuals / groups Working within a team	Working within a community / outreach setting
SKILLS & ABILITIES	Numerate and literate Excellent written and oral communication skills Understanding of principles of Health Promotion Understanding of issues relating to tuberculosis care including adults and children. Understanding of health /social problems of homeless people, including refugees and asylum seekers	Computer literacy
PERSONAL QUALITIES	Committment to the principles of equal opportunities Proven experience of working within a non-discriminatory framework Ability to work constructively within a team and offer support to team members Ability to work on own initiative	
OTHER REQUIREMENTS	A reliable work record	

APPENDIX 3.0

HEALTH PROMOTION MATERIAL

What is tuberculosis?

TB is an ancient disease that has left its traces in Stone Age skeletons and Egyptian mummies. People of all ages, nationalities and social backgrounds can get TB.

TB is caused by a germ (bacterium) called Mycobacterium tuberculosis, which most commonly affects the lungs (called pulmonary TB) and can be infectious. But TB can also affect other parts of the body such as the lymph glands, spine, stomach and brain (called non-pulmonary TB, or extra-pulmonary TB) and is usually non-infectious.

What is drug-resistant tuberculosis?

Drug-resistant TB and multidrug-resistant TB (MDR-TB) are caused when TB germs develop resistance to one or more of the anti-TB drugs. This can be a very serious problem and means that the drug/s can no longer kill the TB bacteria inside the body. Resistance to drugs complicates the treatment, making it necessary to treat with more drugs for a much longer period of time. These drugs may also cause serious side effects and the person with TB may become infectious again, thereby increasing the risk of spreading TB bacteria to other people.

How is TB spread?

TB is spread through the air when people who have infectious TB germs in their lungs cough or sneeze. People who breathe these germs into their lungs can become infected. Although TB is infectious, its spread usually requires prolonged close contact with an infectious person. This means that the most likely people to become infected are those living in the same accommodation or working in close contact.

What is TB infection?

To most individuals who breathe in TB germs and become infected, no immediate illness is caused because their immune system fights the TB and prevents the germs from growing. This means the TB germs are inactive and are not infectious and people may be unaware that they have the infection.

In other cases, people infected with TB overcome the initial infection and remain well for years, but may develop TB disease many years later as a result of a weakened immune system or other serious health problems (called reactivation TB).

What is TB disease?

In some individuals, shortly after becoming infected with TB, the germs become active and cause illness, making the person feel unwell. People more at risk of developing active TB are those with a suppressed immune system, e.g. following organ transplantation; pregnancy; young children; people who live in overcrowded living conditions; the homeless; people with a high intake of alcohol; people using drugs; those with HIV infection and the elderly.

Symptoms of TB

People with TB usually have 3 or more of the following symptoms for 3 or more weeks:
- *A persistent cough - usually with the production of sputum (phlegm)*
- *Sputum - which may contain blood in advanced cases*
- *Sweating at night*
- *Loss of appetite*
- *Weight loss*
- *Loss of energy*

How is TB diagnosed?
There are several methods, such as:
- *Skin test (Heaf / Mantoux)*
- *Chest X-ray*
- *Sputum tests*
- *Blood tests*
- *Assessment of TB risk factors*
- *Sample of tissue for examination.*

How is TB treated?
TB is treated by taking a combination of TB tablets (antibiotics) usually for a period of 6 months, but in some cases longer. TB can be cured completely but only if the medication is taken regularly and for the full course. People who have other health problems (e.g. HIV or diabetes) usually respond just as well to TB treatment.

Depending on individual circumstances, those with infectious TB might be admitted to isolation in hospital for the initial two weeks of treatment in order to monitor their progress. In other cases, some might be treated at home and followed-up regularly by the TB Service. Under normal circumstances, after taking treatment for 2 weeks, people should no longer be infectious and should remain so as long as they are taking their TB medication as prescribed.

Therefore, it is very important that people do not stop taking their medication when they are feeling well again because it can be dangerous for their health. If a person stops taking medicine before their doctor or nurse tells them that it is safe to do so, the TB germs will grow again and the germs may also become resistant to one or more of the TB drugs (called drug-resistant TB).

To promote a full recovery, Specialist TB Nurses provide advice and support on a regular basis throughout treatment. Directly Observed Therapy (DOT) is one method of helping to complete treatment - this means receiving medication and support from a nominated healthcare worker.

How is TB prevented?
- *The most important way of preventing the spread of TB is to identify and successfully treat those with TB disease.*
- *It is important to identify and screen close contacts of people with TB (known as the 'index case') to establish whether they have been infected with TB. Another reason for screening contacts is that, even if the index case is not infectious, one of the contacts may have infectious TB and needs to be treated.*
- *Screening of those who are at high risk of TB.*
- *Education about the signs and symptoms of, and treatment for, TB.*
- *BCG vaccination is usually given to children between 10-14 years of age and at some hospitals babies are vaccinated at birth.*
- *Coughing and sneezing into a handkerchief will help to prevent the spread of germs.*

What to do if you are worried about TB
If you are worried about TB infection or disease, or if you think you may be developing symptoms of TB, you should contact your doctor (GP) or healthcare worker.

[Written by Marais F., Keogh S. & O' Donoghue M., 2000 for Tb Network]

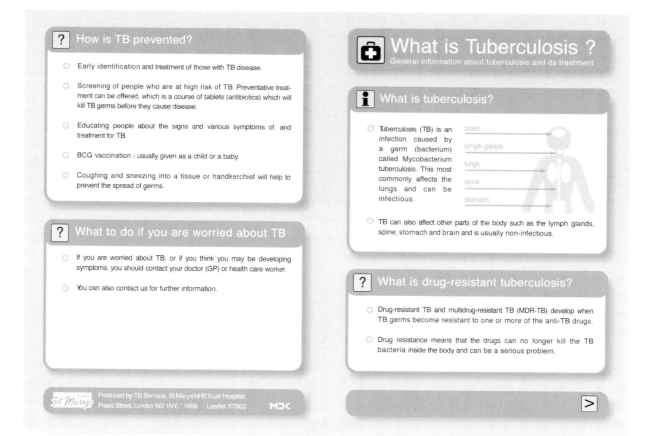

[?] How is TB prevented?

- Early identification and treatment of those with TB disease.

- Screening of people who are at high risk of TB. Preventative treatment can be offered, which is a course of tablets (antibiotics) which will kill TB germs before they cause disease.

- Educating people about the signs and various symptoms of, and treatment for TB.

- BCG vaccination - usually given as a child or a baby.

- Coughing and sneezing into a tissue or handkerchief will help to prevent the spread of germs.

[?] What to do if you are worried about TB

- If you are worried about TB, or if you think you may be developing symptoms, you should contact your doctor (GP) or health care worker.

- You can also contact us for further information.

St Marys Produced by TB Service, St Marys NHS Trust Hospital, Praed Street, London W2 1NY. ' 1999   Leaflet XTB03   MDK

[+] What is Tuberculosis ?
General information about tuberculosis and its treatment

[i] What is tuberculosis?

- Tuberculosis (TB) is an infection caused by a germ (bacterium) called Mycobacterium tuberculosis. This most commonly affects the lungs and can be infectious.

  brain
  lymph glands
  lungs
  spine
  stomach

- TB can also affect other parts of the body such as the lymph glands, spine, stomach and brain and is usually non-infectious.

[?] What is drug-resistant tuberculosis?

- Drug-resistant TB and multidrug-resistant TB (MDR-TB) develop when TB germs become resistant to one or more of the anti-TB drugs.

- Drug resistance means that the drugs can no longer kill the TB bacteria inside the body and can be a serious problem.

[>]

[+] General information about the medicine you may be given

Drug	Description	Possible side effects
RIFAMPICIN	150mg red and blue/grey capsule 300mg red and pink capsule	This capsule will colour your urine, tears and sperm orange. People who wear contact lenses should wear glasses until treatment has completed. The contraceptive pill will not work effectively - and an alternative method of contraception is recommended. There could be changes in your liver function. You may experience skin rashes, vomiting or diarrhoea.
ISONIAZID	100mg round white tablet 50 mg small round white tablet	This tablet may cause nausea, vomiting and tingling in the hands and feet, (PYRIDOXINE is given to prevent this).
PYRAZINAMIDE	500mg round white tablet (larger than the isoniazid)	This tablet may cause rashes, nausea, vomiting, jaundice, fevers, aches or pains in joints.
ETHAMBUTOL	400mg round and grey tablet 100mg yellow tablet	These tablets can cause blurred vision, disturbance in red and green colour vision. Any visual disturbances should be reported immediately.
PYRIDOXINE (vitamin B6)	50mg small round white tablet	This tablet usually does not cause any side effects.
RIFINAH combines rifampicin + isoniazid	300mg orange capsule shaped tablet 150mg round bright pink tablet	Both these tablets contain RIFAMPICIN and ISONIAZID. Side effects as above.
RIFATER combines rifampicin, isoniazid, + pyrazinamide	Round light pink tablet	Contains RIFAMPICIN, ISONIAZID, and PYRAZINAMIDE. Side effects as above.

[?] If you have any questions about your medicine please ask the TB nurses, doctor or pharmacist!

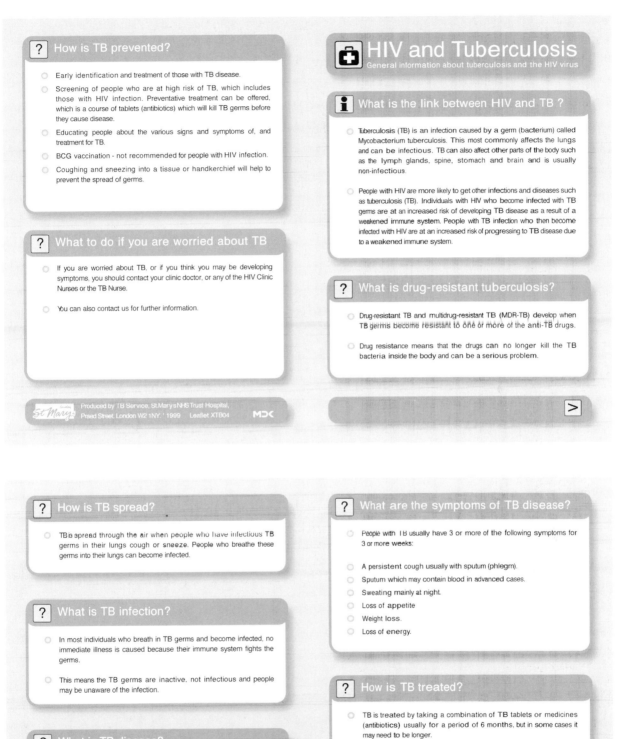

How is TB prevented?

- Early identification and treatment of those with TB disease.
- Screening of people who are at high risk of TB, which includes those with HIV infection. Preventative treatment can be offered, which is a course of tablets (antibiotics) which will kill TB germs before they cause disease.
- Educating people about the various signs and symptoms of, and treatment for TB.
- BCG vaccination - not recommended for people with HIV infection.
- Coughing and sneezing into a tissue or handkerchief will help to prevent the spread of germs.

What to do if you are worried about TB

- If you are worried about TB, or if you think you may be developing symptoms, you should contact your clinic doctor, or any of the HIV Clinic Nurses or the TB Nurse.
- You can also contact us for further information.

Produced by TB Service, St.Marys NHS Trust Hospital, Praed Street, London W2 1NY. ' 1999   Leaflet XTB04

HIV and Tuberculosis
General information about tuberculosis and the HIV virus

What is the link between HIV and TB ?

- Tuberculosis (TB) is an infection caused by a germ (bacterium) called Mycobacterium tuberculosis. This most commonly affects the lungs and can be infectious. TB can also affect other parts of the body such as the lymph glands, spine, stomach and brain and is usually non-infectious.
- People with HIV are more likely to get other infections and diseases such as tuberculosis (TB). Individuals with HIV who become infected with TB germs are at an increased risk of developing TB disease as a result of a weakened immune system. People with TB infection who then become infected with HIV are at an increased risk of progressing to TB disease due to a weakened immune system.

What is drug-resistant tuberculosis?

- Drug-resistant TB and multidrug-resistant TB (MDR-TB) develop when TB germs become resistant to one or more of the anti-TB drugs.
- Drug resistance means that the drugs can no longer kill the TB bacteria inside the body and can be a serious problem.

>

How is TB spread?

- TB is spread through the air when people who have infectious TB germs in their lungs cough or sneeze. People who breathe these germs into their lungs can become infected.

What is TB infection?

- In most individuals who breath in TB germs and become infected, no immediate illness is caused because their immune system fights the germs.
- This means the TB germs are inactive, not infectious and people may be unaware of the infection.

What is TB disease?

- Individuals who overcome the initial infection may develop TB disease many years later as a result of a weakened immune system caused by HIV infection.
- Others infected by HIV may develop TB disease shortly after being infected with TB.

What are the symptoms of TB disease?

- People with TB usually have 3 or more of the following symptoms for 3 or more weeks:
- A persistent cough usually with sputum (phlegm).
- Sputum which may contain blood in advanced cases.
- Sweating mainly at night.
- Loss of appetite
- Weight loss.
- Loss of energy.

How is TB treated?

- TB is treated by taking a combination of TB tablets or medicines (antibiotics) usually for a period of 6 months, but in some cases it may need to be longer.
- TB can be cured completely, including people infected with HIV, but only if the medication is taken as prescribed for the full course.
- If TB tablets are not taken for the full course, the germs will grow again and may become drug resistant to one or more of the TB drugs (called drug-resistant TB). TB that is resistant to some of the medicine is more difficult to treat and may require more time to be treated successfully.

Remember - Tuberculosis can be cured if the correct medication is taken for whole course.

ℹ Important information

- Take your medicine every day without missing doses, but if you do forget, inform the TB nurse or doctor or pharmacist.
- All medication must be taken orally.
- Try to take all of your TB tablets together on an empty stomach (30 minutes before food) to improve absorption.
- Remember to attend your appointments with the TB nurses so that your treatment can be monitored and you can receive more medication.
- If you lose or run out of medication please contact the TB nurses, doctor or pharmacist immediately.
- Remember to inform the TB nurses, doctor or pharmacist if you are taking any other medicine or drugs, prescribed or non prescribed, because they could interact with your TB preventative medication.
- Keep all medication out of the reach of children.
- Store all medicines in a dry, cool place unless otherwise informed.
- Remember to inform the TB nurses, doctor or pharmacist if you have any side effects or concerns or questions about your medication.

✚ Additional information

St.Mary's Produced by TB Service, St.Mary's NHS Trust Hospital, Praed Street, London W2 1NY. ' 1999 Leaflet XTB01 MJ<

✚ Preventative treatment for TB
Information about treatment that prevents TB disease

? Why you have to take this medicine

- You have been infected with tuberculosis (TB) but you are not infectious.
- By taking the medication every day as prescribed the TB germs will be prevented from developing into disease.
- Although you are feeling well it is important that you do not miss any doses and complete the prescribed course.

🕐 How long is the treatment for?

- Treatment for TB is usually three to six months, however it may be shorter or longer depending on your health and whether you are taking any other medication. This will be discussed with you by your doctor and TB nurse.
- It is important that the medicine is taken as prescribed for the full course to make sure all the TB bacteria (germs) are killed.
- If you do not take your tablets, the TB germs may develop into TB disease.

>

✚ General information about the medicine you may be given

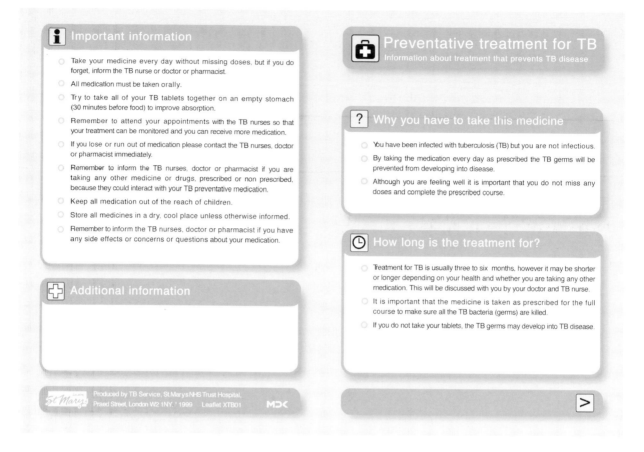

Drug		Description	Possible side effects
ISONIAZID		100mg round white tablet 50 mg small round white tablet	This tablet may cause nausea, vomiting and tingling in the hands and feet. (PYRIDOXINE is given to prevent this).
RIFAMPICIN		150mg red and blue/grey capsule 300mg red and pink capsule	This capsule will colour your urine, tears and sperm orange. People who wear contact lenses should wear glasses until treatment has completed. The contraceptive pill will not work effectively - and an alternative method of contraception is recommended. There could be changes in your liver function. You may experience skin rashes, vomiting or diarrhoea.
PYRAZINAMIDE		500mg round white tablet (larger than the isoniazid)	This tablet may cause rashes, nausea, vomiting, jaundice, fevers, aches or pains in joints.
PYRIDOXINE (vitamin B6)		50mg small round white tablet	This tablet usually does not cause any side effects.
RIFINAH combines rifampicin + isoniazid		300mg orange capsule shaped tablet 150mg round bright pink tablet	Both these tablets contain RIFAMPICIN and ISONIAZID. Side effects as above.

? If you have any questions about your medicine please ask the TB nurses, doctor or pharmacist!

APPENDIX 4.0

GUIDELINES: OUTREACH WORK ASSIGNMENTS

GUIDELINES FOR OUTREACH WORK

THE PRIME AIM OF THESE GUIDELINES IS:

To ensure the *safety* of team members and patients/clients when undertaking outreach duties in the community.

THE PRINCIPLE OBJECTIVES IN UNDERTAKING OUTREACH WORK ARE:

1. To make domicilliary visits in order to check progress.

2. To make domicilliary visits in order to monitor compliance (e.g tablet checks).

3. To make domicilliary visits in order to assess potential barriers to compliance.

4. To trace non-attenders and encourage them to reattend the TB Service.

5. To assess undeclared contacts, i.e potential infectious cases.

6. To provide support for those on anti-TB therapy.

7. To assess patients' health needs within their own social environment.

8. To facilitate enhancement of the health of those on anti-MTB therapy.

PRINCIPLE GUIDELINES:

The *safety* of outreach workers is of prime importance *at all times*. Avoiding confrontational or potentially dangerous situations is crucial to the success of outreach activity. It is important that outreach workers adhere to the following principal guidelines *at all times*:

1. Team members should feel *safe* and *comfortable* whilst undertaking outreach activities. If at any time they feel 'threatened' or 'uneasy', they should discontinue the assignment and return immediately to the office.

2. If there is any cause for concern about the safety of outreach workers when planning an assignment, a discussion should take place with the 'Manager & Lead Nurse', or in his/her absence the General Manager: Medicine, and a decision made as to whether:

   - No outreach duty should be undertaken.

   - The patient / client should be seen only at St. Mary's Hospital.

   - A visit with police escort should be undertaken.

3. Outreach assignments are identified according to patient and service needs. Accordingly, outreach duties could be carried out during Clinic times on any day from Monday to Friday and workers should be *strict* about *keeping to time*.

4. Prior to each outreach session, the 'Manager & Lead Nurse', or in his/her absence another TB Nurse Specialist (on duty cover), must be informed with the address/es and telephone number/s of outreach assignments including expected time of return. In the absence of the 'Manager & Lead Nurse' and another TB Nurse Specialist to provide on duty cover, the 'General Manager: Medicine', or in her/his absence the 'Lead Consultant', must be informed with the above details.

5. Outreach work should be conducted, preferably, during Clinic times only. However, if an after-hours assignment is needed, the 'Manager & Lead Nurse' or the person on duty cover, should be informed. At the end of the session, workers should *always* page either the 'Manager & Lead Nurse' or the person on duty cover to inform them of their safe return home.

6. Ideally, outreach should be conducted by a *minimum of two people* - the second person does not necessarily have to be a TB Nurse Specialist but could be another worker involved in the patient / client's care,

e.g. District Nurse, Social Worker, etc. This is for personal safety both of workers and patients, for support and to allow for reflective evaluation and monitoring of common issues. However, if a second person is not available, and / or the TB Nurse feels safe and comfortable with undertaking the outreach on her / his own, the specific assignment should be discussed with the TB Nurse team prior to the staff member leaving St. Mary's Hospital.

7. *Identifications* should be carried *at all times*, together with the TB Service list of phone numbers. These are confidential and should be kept in a safe place at all times where patients cannot gain access to them.

8. The *mobile phone* must be carried by outreach workers on all outreach assignments *at all times*. It is the responsibility of the individual outreach workers to ensure they understand how to use the phone.

9. Outreach workers should *not separate* during an assignment, even if talking to separate patients. Always remain within close visual contact of one another.

10. Clear *professional boundaries* should be maintained at all times. It is important to be aware that we are working in patients'/clients' territory and to be sensitive to this while maintaining a professional delivery of service. At all times, be aware of, and sensitive to, the cultural and religious practices of patients / clients. If something, someone or a situation does not feel comfortable then *do not* do it and *withdraw*.

11. Related to the above point, at *no time* should outreach workers accept anything, gift or otherwise from patients/clients and at *no time* should workers give patients/clients money directly.

12. If members of the public want to know who we are, workers should explain that we are from a health project - *maintain the confidentiality* of patients at all times.

13. In the event of an emergency during the course of outreach activity, the police should be informed if staff safety is threatened. Otherwise, leave the area as quickly as possible, return to St. Mary's and inform the 'Manager & Lead Nurse' or person on duty cover.

14. In the event of car breakdown or delay on public transport system; inform the 'Manager & Lead Nurse' or person on duty cover.

15. At the end of *all* outreach sessions, on arrival back at the hospital, workers should always inform the 'Manager & Lead Nurse' or person on duty cover of their return.

16. On returning to the office at the end of all outreach assignments, workers should update the relevant patients' notes.

17. Outreach workers who use cars should ensure that they display a BMA sticker and an official notification of outreach status. The TB Service cannot at any time take responsibility for illegal parking. At *no time* should contacts or known patients/clients be allowed into the vehicle.

18. When using public transport for outreach assignments, where possible, travel cards should be purchased and retained for submission to the 'Manager & Lead Nurse' for refund from the Directorate.

19. In the event of an emergency during outreach, the mobile phone should be used to contact the appropriate emergency service. Clinically qualified outreach workers should ensure that their appropriate professional bodies (eg. the RCN) cover them for administration of emergency medical treatment.

PROBLEM SHOOTING

If outreach workers have not returned **1 hour** after their expected time of arrival in the office, or have not made contact via the mobile phone when an after-hours assignment has been undertaken, it will be the responsibility of the 'Manager & Lead Nurse' or the person on duty cover to be aware of this and to carry out the following:

1. Contact the outreach workers on the **mobile phone [Tel:].**

2. Check where outreach workers were last and find out what time they left.

3. Inform the General Manager: Medicine or in her/his absence the Lead Consultant.

4. If the workers have not been located, inform the police.

5. Inform the On-Call manager for the Trust.

HEALTH & SAFETY

1. As previously stated, the health and safety of both outreach workers and patients / clients is of **prime** concern during **all** outreach activities.

2. Outreach workers should be familiar with the St. Mary's Hospital NHS Trust policy on 'Health & Safety' and follow it **at all times**.

3. Clinically qualified staff have a legal and professional responsibility to respond to **any** medical related emergency while undertaking duties for St. Mary's, including outreach. They should therefore ensure that they are familiar with and regularly updated on resuscitation guidelines and also ensure adequate liability cover via their professional bodies (eg. the RCN).

COMPLAINTS

1. Any complaints made by patients / clients should initially be dealt with immediately upon receipt by the outreach worker who fields the complaint. The worker should follow established Trust guidelines and try to resolve the issue there and then.

2. For more serious complaints or allegations (eg. against another worker) patients / clients should be directed to forward the complaint to the 'Manager & Lead Nurse' or the General Manager: Medical Directorate.

3. During investigation of such complaints the patient / client's confidentiality should be maintained as far as possible, but it should be explained to them that occasionally they may need to be identified for an investigation to proceed.

UNDER NO CIRCUMSTANCES SHOULD A MEMBER OF STAFF KNOWINGLY PLACE THEMSELVES AT UNNECESSARY RISK.

APPENDIX 5.0

GUIDELINES: TRANSPORTATION OF ANTI-TB DRUGS

GUIDELINES FOR TRANSPORTATION OF ANTI-MTB DRUGS

THE PRIME AIM OF THESE GUIDELINES IS:

1 To ensure the safety of team members and patients / clients.

2. To prevent any litigation against members of staff or Trust.

PROCEDURE FOR TRANSPORTING ANTI-MTB DRUGS TO PATIENTS / CLIENTS IN THE COMMUNITY:

1. All TB Nurse Specialists must follow the 'Principle Guidelines' as outlined in 'Guidelines for Outreach Work' [see Appendix 4, page 69].

2. All drugs being transported to the patient / client's home should be prescribed, clearly labelled and up to date.

3. Before leaving the hospital, check that all drugs are correctly dispensed.

4. Document names of drugs, dose and quantity / length of supply in patients' notes (TB Nurse Documentation).

5. Drugs should be packaged in an inconspicuous way to avoid unwanted interest or identification.

PROCEDURE FOR RETURNING ANTI-MTB DRUGS TO THE HOSPITAL:

1. If the patient / client is not at home, the drugs should be returned to St. Mary's and kept either in the drugs cupboard in the Chest & Allergy Clinic or in the Jefferiss Wing pharmacy (for patients co-infected with HIV).

2. In the event that certain anti-MTB drugs are no longer used by patients / clients, they should be advised to return such drugs to the Clinic at their next appointment. In these circumstances, the TB Nurse Specialist should return the drugs to either the Outpatient or Jefferiss Wing Pharmacy.

3. Alternatively, the TB Nurse Specialist may collect drugs that are no longer used by patients / clients and return them to either the Outpatient or Jefferiss Wing Pharmacy.

PROCEDURE IN THE EVENT THAT DRUGS ARE LOST:

1. Inform the 'Manager & Lead Nurse' - or in his/her absence the 'General Manager: Medicine' or if not available, the 'Lead Consultant' - at the earliest opportunity.

2. Inform the Pharmacy from where the anti-MTB drugs were dispensed and rearrange another script.

3. In addition, if the drugs were stolen, complete an Incident Form and inform the Chief Pharmacist at the earliest opportunity.

ACKNOWLEDGEMENTS

SERVICE DEVELOPMENT

HEALTH PROVIDERS

The author would like to acknowledge and thank the following people for their support and contributions in the development of this Nurse-led Service: (names in alphabetical order)

Dr Richard Coker	*Trust Lead Physician: TB & HIV/TB, St. Mary's Hospital*
Dr Onn Min Kon	*Trust Lead Physician: TB, St. Mary's Hospital*
Dr Kai Lau	*Consultant Communicable Disease Control, KCW HA*
Dr David Mitchell	*Medical Director, St. Mary's Hospital*
Professor Rory Shaw	*Consultant Physician: Chest Medicine, St. Mary's Hospital*
Dr Graham Taylor	*Lead Physician: HIV/TB, St. Mary's Hospital*
Dr Sam Walters	*Lead Physician: Paediatrics/TB, St. Mary's Hospital*
Prof Jonathan Weber	*Chair, Control of Infection Committee, St. Mary's Hospital*
Sheena Basnayake	*TB Clinical Nurse Specialist, St. Mary's Hospital*
Cathleen Battoo	*Outreach TB Nurse for Pilot Project, St. Mary's Hospital*
Jeanette Bennett	*TB Clinical Nurse Specialist, St. Mary's Hospital*
Malcolm Cocksedge	*TB Nurse Specialist, St. Mary's Hospital*
Gini Gleissberg	*TB Nurse Specialist, St. Mary's Hospital*
Gwen Hay	*TB Clinical Nurse Specialist, St. Mary's Hospital*
Samantha Libertino	*TB Clinical Nurse Specialist, St. Mary's Hospital*
Sarah Myers	*TB Nurse Specialist, St. Mary's Hospital*
Marie O'Donoghue	*TB Clinical Nurse Specialist, St. Mary's Hospital*
Ellie Prosser	*TB Clinical Nurse Specialist, St. Mary's Hospital*
Theresa Shryane	*TB Clinical Nurse Specialist, St. Mary's Hospital*
Susan Yates	*TB Clinical Nurse Specialist, St. Mary's Hospital*
Mandy Field	*Business Manager HIV/GUM Directorate, St. Mary's Hospital*
Sheila Jones	*Deputy Director of Nursing, St. Mary's Hospital*
Sue Lyons	*Director of Nursing, St. Mary's Hospital*
Pat McCann	*Chief Executive, St. Mary's Hospital*
Terina Riches	*General Manager, Medical Directorate, St. Mary's Hospital*
Carol Toogood	*Directorate Nurse Manager: Medicine, St. Mary's Hospital*
Claire Brain	*Dietician: HIV/TB, St. Mary's Hospital*
Catherine Mooney	*Chief Pharmacist, St. Mary's Hospital*
Stuart Philip	*Bacteriology, St. Mary's Hospital*
Rosie Weston	*Senior HIV Pharmacist, St. Mary's Hospital*

PATIENTS & SERVICE USERS

Special thanks go to all to those individuals directly affected by tuberculosis who shared their experiences and expressed suggestions for improved service provision, access and uptake.

SERVICE PLANNING VISITS TO THE USA

The author would like to acknowledge and thank all the organisations and specialist staff for their advice, support and guidance, including all the literature and educational materials:

Bureau of Tuberculosis Control, The City of New York Department of Health, New York City
TB Control Division, Department of Public Health, City and County of San Francisco, San Francisco
Tuberculosis Control, Health & Human Services Agency, County of San Diego, San Diego

PUBLICATION REVIEW & COMMENTS

The author would like to thank Dr Richard Coker, Dr Tony Ellam, Prof. Nancy Gibson, Mark King, Dr Vanessa Graham, Samantha Libertino, Marie O'Donoghue, and Theresa Shaw and Carol Toogood for support, comments and suggestions.

SPONSORS

MƆK